V.S. NAIPAUL

THE INDIAN TRILOGY

V.S. NAIPAUL
THE INDIAN TRILOGY

Namrata Rathore Mahanta

ATLANTIC
PUBLISHERS & DISTRIBUTORS

Published by

ATLANTIC
PUBLISHERS & DISTRIBUTORS
B-2, Vishal Enclave Opp. Rajouri Garden,
New Delhi-110027
Phones : 25413460, 25429987, 25466842

Sales Office
7/22, Ansari Road, Darya Ganj,
New Delhi–110002
Phones : 23273880, 23275880, 23280451
Fax : 91-11-23285873
web : www.atlanticbooks.com
e-mail : info@atlanticbooks.com

ISBN 81-269-0349-X

Printed in India
at Nice Printing Press, Delhi

To

Professor Sushila Singh

Preface

Diasporic consciousness in the world of literature is becoming an increasingly dominant phenomenon. It is the mental flight of a people constantly trying to reconstruct their present from a past that is lost to them. Their roots shoot down only to strike against a frozen, fractured consciousness and then begin a search for crevasses—to anchor on to, and the diasporic literature is born. Although many individual and comparative studies have been conducted on the writers of the Indian diaspora, there is a dearth of studies that analyze this phenomenon as the growth of an individual writer within the framework of his continuing encounters with his homeland. V.S. Naipaul's unique position as a 'twice removed' diasporic writer and his three books spanning three decades of his engagement with India provide this unprecedented opportunity.

The genesis of diaspora, its penetration of the writer's consciousness, and the resultant sensibility that gives birth to cross-cultural writing is the context in which Naipaul's Janus-faced relationship with India is analyzed. This turbulent relationship finds expression in Naipaul's deep-seated concern for the land of his ancestors. His vision being coloured by the very same diasporic consciousness that birthed his quest, he is caught within the ripples of his own making in his first real encounter with India.

Naipaul's initial bitterness generated a unique sense of detachment, which in addition to being essential to any original quest has yielded transparency to his struggle to establish a connection with India. He has attempted to understand the country against its cultural backdrop and has made a well-ordered search for the roots of the maladies that ail India, which in turn has led him to seek the vast possibilities offered by the non-fiction narrative mode. Thus Naipaul's writings on India are not only the outcome of his quest for India but are also a unique record of the making of a diasporic writer, of his development, of his anguish, rage, search, and finally of his successful mental restoration of India from a pattern of painful fragmentation to wholeness.

Naipaul's three books on India: *An Area of Darkness* (1964), *India: A Wounded Civilization* (1977), and *India: A Million Mutinies Now* (1990) are central to this analysis. I do not wish to introduce the dilution of dwelling at length on the Indian Diaspora in the Caribbean and its attempts at dealing with its Indian past. Although I recognize the currency of this phenomenon and occasionally invoke the same in my study, I have refrained from writing excessively on this already much discussed aspect of the Diaspora. I have instead focused on the tensions and forces at work between the diasporic writer and the country of his ancestors.

This book attempts to study how Naipaul finally resolves his problematic equation with India. Naipaul's earlier vituperation against Indian culture and politics emerges to form a part of his diasporic worldview. By reading these works as diasporic writings and as a series we can perceive the maturing of Naipaul's diasporic consciousness.

Namrata Rathore Mahanta

ACKNOWLEDGMENTS

I shall always remain indebted to Professor Sushila Singh for her constant guidance and advice and for standing by me like a rock in time of personal and professional crises. I cannot thank her enough so I dedicate this work to her.

My grateful thanks to the Banaras Hindu University where this book first emerged as a Ph.D dissertation. My heartfelt thanks to my teachers in the Department of English, B.H.U. who have contributed so much over the years to my appreciation and understanding of literature. I am grateful to Professor A.K. Tripathy whose enthusiasm and good humour saw me through troubled patches. My special thanks are due to Professor A.K. Singh, Head of the Department of English, Saurashtra University, Rajkot for his invaluable insight and suggestions. Professor K.P. Singh, Centre of Advance Study in Botany, Banaras Hindu University, Varanasi has been a constant source of encouragement and has extended useful tips throughout the course of my work. I wish to express my respect and gratitude to him.

For facilitating literature survey, I extend my thanks to the Sayaji Rao Gaekwad Library, Banaras Hindu University, Varanasi; the Indo-American Centre for International Studies, Hyderabad; the Central Institute of Foreign Languages, Hyderabad; British Council Libraries at New Delhi and Kolkata and the National Library, Kolkata.

My sincere gratitude to my parents for nurturing my dreams and for having brought me up to believe in myself above everything, in spite of everything. With profound love, I acknowledge the selfless concern and help of Ma, Baba and Chachi. My affectionate thanks to Bani, Amar, Bithin, Puja, Sweety, Vandana and Payel for helping me in every possible way and to my son Aaditya for cheerfully putting up with my absences.

Contents

ABBREVIATIONS

An Area of Darkness	*AD*
India: A Wounded Civilization	*WC*
India: A Million Mutinies Now	*MM*
Finding the Centre	*FC*
The Enigma of Arrival	*EOA*

1

THE MAKING OF THE WRITER

> Writing is a process of learning. The writer writes himself into an understanding of his world and it has taken me many years and much writing to arrive at the understanding, which I now have.
>
> V.S. Naipaul, Interview with Tarun Tejpal.

Imperialism fractured the world. It was responsible for mass dislocation of people and consequently of cultures. Third world diasporic writing is rooted in the postcolonial situation. It is governed by an urge to relocate, to reconstitute, and most importantly, to establish and examine cultural identity. Cultural identity in itself being a derivative of historical and political circumstance, it naturally follows that diasporic writing be densely interwoven with journeys to one's roots. To be a part of Diaspora is to be trapped within complex personal circumstance; to be a writer in addition is to have one's imagination shackled to the collective forces of history, culture and tradition. This complexity emerges as a marked pattern in the creative forces at work in diasporic writers. However, any attempt to define this pattern falters and fails because the same circumstance can evoke varied responses in different writers; it can even evoke varied responses in the same writer with the passage of time. Constant change can therefore be the only common denominator for writers who live through the experience of Diaspora.

The term 'Diaspora' originally referred to the dispersal of Jews as a consequence of the Roman conquest of Jerusalem. The Jews were driven from their homeland and their dispersal became a mass migration. They spread across the

Mediterranean. They reached Spain and Portugal and even far off Poland and Russia. Wherever they went, they distinguished themselves in various fields. After the conquest of Granada and their consequent expulsion from Spain, they embarked on long voyages across the Atlantic and landed in Venice, in Holland, and on the African coast. History is replete with the horrors of organized violence against this race. Facing persecution unparalleled in history, the Jews not only survived but also preserved their racial and cultural integrity and their rituals. Theirs is the only case of Diasporas returning to their ancient homeland. They also revived their ancient language, Hebrew. The Jewish Diaspora is therefore the original model for all studies of Diaspora. However, the restoration of Israel is an exceptional case of realization of the Diaspora's dream of a return to their homeland. Generally, the Diasporas can never return to their homeland because 'homeland' for them is a series of mental images, often highly eulogized. Therefore, when a physical return to the homeland lays bare the chasm between their image and the visible reality, it fails to produce a mental equivalent of their physical return. Their alienation is thus doubled. Hydra-headed questions of ethnicity, nationality and migrancy only add to its complications.

It is impossible to put forward an empirical definition of Diaspora. Diasporic space is never one's natural space. It is the space that has to be painfully negotiated between the overwhelming contradictions of ethnicity, religion, nationalities and nationalisms. Chaotic occurrences on the global scenario have forced us to stand face-to-face with these contradictions: ethnic cleansing in Bosnia Herzegovina, the breaking up of the Soviet Union and Yugoslavia, Idi Amin's open attack on Ugandan Asians, clashes between the Black population and Indian population in Trinidad, between Israel and Palestine, and the coups in Fiji. The latest of the Fijian coups led by George Speight and his violent ethnic Fijian supporters ousted the Mahendra Chaudhry government and launched a campaign against the Indo-Fijian population. It was a replay of the violence against Indo-Fijians, which had followed the 1987 coup led by Col. Sitiveni Rabuka and the highly discriminatory 1990 constitution. It was only seven years later in 1997 that a new constitution upheld multiethnic democracy. Fiji's Court of Appeal's validation of the 1997 constitution has given the final verdict against the ethnic demon created by the likes of George Speight but for how long? How long will it take before the ethnic demon stalks the islands once again? It is in this context that Salman Rushdie has articulated the questions of migrancy, roots and the ownership of land. In an article on the coup in Fiji he writes:

> ...the fundamentals of the land question have been thoroughly obscured. The truth is that after 100 years, Fiji's Indians have every right to think of themselves as being, and to be treated as being, fully as Fijian as ethnic Fijians.[1]

Ironically, even after a century of staying and working on Fijian soil, Indo-Fijians are prevented from owning land on the main island. They hold it on a ninety-nine year lease, which the Speight coup proposed to annul as and when these expired. Over the years since 1987, the Indo-Fijian Diaspora has been slowly moving to Australia and New Zealand. One day or the other, questions of land and home are bound to erupt at these new sites too. "Migrant peoples do not remain visitors forever," says Rushdie. "In the end, their new land owns them as once their old land did, and they have a right to own it in their turn."[2] In stark contrast to the predicament of Indo-Fijians, a copper plate plaque at the Apravasi Ghat[3] at Port Louis in Mauritius declares in Abhimanyu Unnuth's words:

> History turning a blind eye bore him no witness. History standing mute told not his full story.
>
> He who first had watered this land with his sweat and turned stone into fields of gold. The first immigrant, he, son of this land, he was mine, he was yours, he was our very own.[4]

The term 'Diaspora' refers to a matrix of political and social concerns whose interdependence needs to be analysed and studied to combat the tensions that are tearing at the humanitarian values of the world and exposing societies to extreme traumas. At the onset a distinction needs to be made between the uprooted intellectuals, writers and the nameless uprooted masses. Next, a distinction needs to be made within the former category on the basis of circumstance: those moving for reasons of intellectual affinity, those escaping oppression in their homeland, political dissidents and the waifs of colonialism.

The origin of the twentieth century uprooted intellectual can be traced back to Anaxagoras (500 BC—428 BC). Anaxagoras was a Greek philosopher who left his homeland to live in Athens. His doctrines offended the Athenians and he was banished. Empedocles, Ovid, Dante, Hobbes, Victor Hugo, Spinoza—all belong to the category of uprooted intellectuals. Diasporas continually reinvent their circumstances and in doing so they form their own history. The cultural sediment that survives the chain of movements forms the modes of narrative. William Safran has characterized the Diaspora on the basis of cultural sedimentation:

> (1) they or their ancestors, have been dispersed from a specific original 'centre' to two or more peripheral regions; (2) they retain a collective memory, vision or myth about their original homeland—its physical location, history and achievements; (3) they believe that they are not—and perhaps cannot be fully accepted by their host society and therefore feel partly alienated and insulated from it; (4) they regard their ancestral homeland as their true, ideal home and as the place to which they or their descendants would eventually return—when conditions are appropriate; (5) they believe that they should collectively, be committed to the maintenance or restoration of their homeland and to its safety and prosperity; and (6) they continue to relate personally or vicariously to that homeland in one way or the other, and their ethnocommunal consciousness and solidarity are importantly defined by the existence of such a relationship.[5]

This characterization is disputed by Vijay Mishra who holds that "Safran's characterization does not take into account precisely those points at which ethnicity and diasporas part company."[6] He argues that Safran's characterization takes for granted the existence of an exclusive and pure community whereas Diasporas are the result of confluence with the host society and it is the "creation of its own political myths rather than the real possibilities of a return to a homeland," which is its actual characteristic.[7] In the creation of their own political selves, the Diasporas have pushed issues of nationalism, nation and nationhood to the forefront and have reminded us of what Renan had said about national identity—for a unit to rise and take on the condition of nationhood, it is necessary for all individuals concerned to remember what brings them together and forget what could tear them apart.[8]

Frantz Fanon says that colonialism has given us a legacy of "micronationalisms" whereby the idea of nationalism is split into divisive forces such as territorialism, racism and regionalism. The old colonialism manifests itself in the new order of governance and power patterns are caricatured. Therefore any movement that attempts to reject colonialism must provide a system that breaks away from the old colonial pattern. However, Fanon also warns against an uncritical acceptance of nativism as it can easily degenerate into various kinds of separatisms. Bourgeois assimilation and bourgeois nationalism both lead to a replay of the old colonial pattern. Fanon, therefore, calls for a third alternative, which would criticize the machinery and institutions of colonial rule. Subsequent discussions of nationalism by Anderson and Homi Bhabha resonate with Fanon's observations.[9]

For Anderson, the nation is "an imagined political community." He holds that the ideas of nationalism are "cultural artefacts of a particular kind" and any attempt to understand these must begin with an understanding of how these ideas "came into historical being."[10] The same analogy can be extended to a study of the diasporic brand of nationalism. Farrukh Dhondy has presented an interesting example of the NRI outrage against the NASA's naming of its robot as Gunga Din when a corresponding outrage amidst the resident Indians was absent.[11] There is yet another example of the NRI community swinging into action against the movie 'Eyes Wide Shut' for using sacred chants in a denigrating manner. While India was content with imposing a ban on the movie in India, the NRIs persisted till the controversial chants were removed. This feeling for what is one's own even after years of separation from one's roots is intrinsic to displaced communities and it is interesting to note that this feeling is at times stronger than the feeling amongst rooted communities. A classic example is that of NRIs coming to the rescue of the homeland (India) at a time of great economic crisis during the Prime Ministership of P.V. Narasimha Rao.

Having forsaken their homeland for personal benefit, these communities feel responsible towards the home country. An explanation can be found in Homi Bhabha's definition of the "third space" as a hybrid location rich in turmoil from which "the intersubjective and collective experiences of nationness, community interest or cultural values are negotiated."[12] Bhabha looks upon these "third spaces" as "gatherings" of scattered peoples, of "exiles and émigrés and refugees, gatherings on the edge of 'foreign' cultures;...gathering memories...of other worlds lived retroactively; gathering the past in a ritual of revival; gathering the present."[13] This living on the edge imparts a unique position to such "gatherings" and these are able to "translate the difference between them into a kind of solidarity."[14]

Therefore, the formation of diasporic identity is a big step in the larger transformation of the history of the Diaspora. If a writer enters an engagement with history, he writes himself, book by book into the "hybrid location" that Bhabha speaks of, and then if he goes on, there is a possibility of him writing himself out of the "hybrid location" and achieving a more objective world-view. It is in this sense that this study attempts to read V.S. Naipaul's engagement with the history of India. The question of historical circumstance cannot be wished away just because it is far removed from the present reality. What happens when a third world intellectual stands face-to-face with his historical circumstance? Is it the beginning of further alienation or the beginning of assimilation? These questions have manifested themselves in different ways in different writers. Towards the end of *Culture and Imperialism*, Edward Said attempts an answer by quoting Hugo of St. Victor: "The person who finds his homeland sweet is still a tender beginner; he to whom every soil is as his native one is already strong; but he is perfect to whom the entire world is as a foreign place."[15] Said concludes that although traditions, habitations, languages and cultural geographies cannot be denied, the intellectual should not insist on their differences because "survival in fact is about the connections between things."[16] The realization of one's identity should not create a figure of rupture that separates itself from the other communities.

Michel Foucault's concept of "heterotopia" when applied to Diasporas reveals a new paradigm: Spaces can be divided into socially or politically constructed binaries such as legal/illegal, own/other. Heterotopia refers to the spaces that are governed by these politically and socially constructed binaries as 'other.' These 'other' spaces are spaces of crisis, subjugation, or colonization. Heterotopia when applied to Diasporas immediately sheds its bipolar dimensions and becomes multipolar. Diaspora being the result of the coming together of the 'own' and the 'other' is not a third space outside the realm of own/other. It is the manifestation of a reality, which remains in a state of flux between the settled binaries of own/other and works towards diluting, shifting and displacing these binaries. It thus succeeds in forming Fanon's third alternative of a change that originates with the "wretched of the earth" leaving aside both bourgeois assimilation and bourgeois nationalism. Works of social scientists, philosophers and historians have influenced the work of interdisciplinary theorists that have been discussed so far. The theory of Diaspora traverses these interdisciplinary theories; it seeks to achieve that balance in remembering and forgetting which was advocated by Renan. But the problem does not end there. The trouble is not only in deciding what to forget but also, to paraphrase Anderson, it is a battle to decide who will imagine the community.

Writers in all ages have recorded in their works their own renditions of the community as lived in/imagined by them. Three major writers who worked at a distance from their roots are Henry James, James Joyce and Joseph Conrad. Henry James (1843-1916) left America and settled in Europe in 1875, James Joyce (1882-1941) dissatisfied with the narrowness of Irish Catholicism as he saw it, left Ireland for good but immortalized it in his work. Joseph Conrad (1857-1924) was a child of Polish parents who were exiled to northern Russia. On account of their political sympathies, he lived as a young Polish émigré in France. After the death of his parents, his uncle brought him up. He became a sailor and visited the New World. Later he became a naturalized Briton. Throughout his work there exists a pull between conservative and impulsive reactions to circumstance. His journeys as a sailor were his material and his exilic condition was his vision. "Conrad aimed at fidelity. Fidelity required him to be explicit."[17]

Henry James concerned himself with the effect of the older civilization of Europe on American life in his earliest phase of writing. In his next phase he dwelled on an exclusive study of the English scene but then, in his last three novels he returned to a study of contrasts between American and European character. In the *American Scene* (1906) he records his impressions and responses to America after an absence of nearly twenty years. James Joyce's *Dubliners* presents Dublin in four of its aspects—childhood, adolescence, maturity and public life and he claimed to have written these stories with "scrupulous meanness." *A Portrait of the Artist as a Young Man* is an autobiographical account of the progressive rejection of his environment and his corresponding emergence as an artist. Significantly, it is written in the third person as Joyce steps back and records his development as an artist with total objectivity. In *Ulysses* and later in *Finnegans Wake* Joyce attempts to represent, in one short sequence of events, the entirety of human experience. Joyce rejected all points of view, he rejected the world in which his role as an artist was constricted, but in his writings, he went back to the same world over and over again. The internalising of human experience at various levels had permitted him to 'distance' himself and engage in his activity as an artist with total freedom. Joseph Conrad went around the globe recording societies as he saw them in his novels and stories. He records the exploitation of the non-white world by colonial agents:

> They were conquerors, and for that you want only brute force—nothing to boast of...since your strength is just an accident arising from the weakness of others.... The conquest of the earth, which mostly means the taking it

> away from those who have a different complexion or slightly flatter noses than ourselves, is not a pretty thing when you look into it too much. What redeems it is the idea only.[18]

Peter Nazareth in his essay "Out of Darkness: Conrad and Other Third World Writers," sees Conrad as "sneaking through as a member of Leavis's Great Tradition, actually undermining that tradition."[19] With *Lord Jim* Conrad began writing the modern man's existential plight. He deals with alienation and psychic exile in *Heart of Darkness.* His overwhelming sense of the terror of exile is manifested in different ways in *Nostromo, The Secret Agent* and in *Under Western Eyes.*

Under Western Eyes deals with literal exile and in it Conrad has worked across the conflicts that make up the life of exile as a political and personal condition. *Victory* marks Conrad's triumph over exile. It shows that exile can be dismantled by compassion and love. Conrad wrote of psychic exile, he wrote in English, which was his third language. He proved to be an inspiration to many later writers and was the only writer whom Naipaul acknowledges as his precursor.

Naipaul can be compared to Joyce as a cultural exile as both had left the constrictions of their native lands, both had settled in European metropolises and both used their self-imposed exile and their visions of the societies they had left behind. He can be compared to Henry James as an extra-cognizant exile because like James, his distance from his native land had worked towards making him 'extra-cognizant' of its realities. But it is only Conrad with whom he shares his world and his material. Naipaul's relationship with Conrad is a difficult one and Naipaul has discussed it at length in his essay "Conrad's Darkness."[20] Conrad's being the only influence that he directly recognizes, Conrad holds a special place in the making of Naipaul as a writer and his later paradigm shift from fiction to non-fiction. Naipaul, in his earliest phase of his association with Conrad's work found these not only "elusive" and "impenetrable" but also "flawed" on account of a lack of creative imagination. He found a Conrad novel to be "like a simple film with an elaborate commentary."[21] But at a later stage in the essay he lays bare the construction behind his earliest readings of Conrad:

> But we read at different times for different things. We take to novels our own ideas of what the novel should be; and those ideas are made by our needs...our ideas of our background...we can take a writer's virtues for granted. And his originality, the news he is offering us, can go over our heads.[22]

While searching for his own material, Naipaul discovered that his predecessors had written about "highly organized societies." He also found that he could not follow the same pattern because his colonial world was a disjointed whole. He easily identified this world as "one of the Conradian dark places" and it led to a reinterpretation of Conrad's works. Naipaul now saw Conrad as a writer who had, sixty years ago, seen and "meditated upon" a world that was now his. Therefore, to understand Conrad, Naipaul felt it necessary to "match his experience" and to set aside his preconceived notions of what a novel ought to be. Although Naipaul retained his reservations about the dormancy of Conrad's creative imagination, he records in the essay that he came to value him for his experience:

> Conrad's value to me is that he is someone who sixty to seventy years ago meditated on my world, a world I recognize today. I feel this about no other writer of the century.[23]

He values Conrad for a meticulous and faithful recording of his experience and vision. The essay ends with Naipaul's lament for the death of the novel as a form that recorded the societies of the past era because societies have themselves broken up. He finds the present world passing into the irretrievable past, "unexamined" and "unmeditated on." Naipaul is thus Conrad's successor because both have steadily worked towards recording their observations of peoples and societies of their times. Conrad staked imagination for the sake of conscientious rendering of truth in thought and fact. Faced with a similar situation, Naipaul abandoned the novel form and moved on to non-fiction so that he could faithfully articulate his vision of the multi-layered chaos in the disjointed societies of our times.

The breaking up of societies and the contemporary option of being able to choose one's society has made such a varied permutation and combination of experience and personal circumstance that writing has become an increasingly personal affair. It has found expression in sheer multiplicity of visions that are at odds with each other. This difference is most evident in the conflicting visions of diasporic and stay-at-home writers. It is this difference that sparks between Derek Walcott, Naipaul, Chinua Achebe, George Lamming, and Jean Rhys; it is this difference that lies as a void between Naipaul and R.K. Narayan; between the Rohinton Mistry who wrote *Such a Long Journey* and the one who wrote *A Fine Balance*. It is this difference between Naipaul's India and Nissim Ezekiel's India that has to be first recognized and then explained. It is also the difference between *An Area of Darkness* and *India: A Million Mutinies Now*.

Writers shape their world in their writing and are simultaneously shaped by the world they inhabit. Achebe and Naipaul both have a colonial past and both have made it the subject of their writing. But while Naipaul stands two generations away from his home soil, Achebe is strongly rooted in his homeland. While Naipaul has no allegiance to anything, except to his own vision, Achebe is fiercely African in his. Naipaul sees "half-made societies," Achebe seeks to show his readers that Africa's glorious past is very much retrievable. Achebe's criticism of Naipaul can only be matched with the outburst in Indian literary circles that followed the publication of *An Area of Darkness*.

In sharp contrast to a rooted Achebe is an alienated George Lamming. Lamming and Naipaul have both gone through similar experiences. Both travelled through the Caribbean and also to the land of their ancestors. Naipaul's experiences of the West Indies are recorded in *The Middle Passage* and his visits to India in *An Area of Darkness, India: A Wounded Civilization* and *India: A Million Mutinies Now*. Lamming in *The Pleasures of Exile* has narrated his visit to America and

Africa. Both have explored the history of the West Indies; Naipaul in *The Loss of El Dorado* and Lamming in *Natives of My Person*. Yet, their visions are very different and diametrically opposite. Lamming finds that Naipaul's first three novels "can't move beyond a castrated satire" and sees in him "a colonial, ashamed of his cultural background."[24] Derek Walcott and Jean Rhys also present two contradictory visions. Walcott seeks to reconstruct through imagination what has been lost through history whereas Jean Rhys writes of voids created by things falling apart. Derek Walcott's 1992 Nobel Lecture declares:

> Break a vase and the love that reassembles the fragments is stronger than the love which took its symmetry for granted when it was whole.... Antillean art is this restoration of our shattered histories, our shards of vocabulary, our archipelago becoming a synonym for pieces broken off from the original continent.[25]

In sharp contrast is Jean Rhys's work. In her novels, her heroines are characters of great vitality whose deracinated states leave them lonely and directionless. They are expatriates and are never able to come to terms with the organized societies in the metropolises. They exist in a void. Rhys's most acclaimed *Wide Sargasso Sea* is a reinvention of the story of Rochester's mad wife in *Jane Eyre*. Rhys has portrayed her as a victim of a colonial society that is passing into decadence. The sense of loss reigns supreme. It is thus evident that in spite of the Caribbean connection that they share, Naipaul, Lamming, Rhys and Walcott are strikingly dissimilar in their visions. This is how the individual conditions of creative writers determine their vision of a society that is not a unified whole but exists in parts and fragments within the writers' lived-in experience. Naipaul's portrayal of the predicament of Mohun Biswas crystallizes this fragmentation:

> His freedom was over, and it had been false. The past could not be ignored; it was never counterfeit; he carried it within himself. If there was a place for him, it was one that had already been hollowed out by time, by everything he had lived through, however imperfect....[26]

It is within this framework of lived-in experience that the writers of the Indian Diaspora are discussed. The diasporic concerns which make Naipaul stand apart from the rest in what seems to be on the surface, a love-hate relationship with India are subsequently brought out.

The original force behind the creation of the Indian Diaspora was the economics of imperialism. After the abolition of the slave trade, Indians were looked upon as the next best non-expensive labour force that could easily be used to substitute the slaves who had worked in British colonies in the Caribbean, the South-Pacific, Singapore, Canada, and Africa. Indians were taken to these colonies in large numbers under a contract. This began in the nineteenth century and continued well into the twentieth century. At a time when 'crossing the black waters' could lead to social ostracization, the acceptance of indenture could not have possibly been a happy choice. It was bound to have been made under extreme constraints. It was a process involving immense pain and it changed the sensibility of these transported people for good. It changed their idea of their homeland and it changed their idea of themselves.[27] Bhikhu Parekh has lauded the typically malleable nature of Indian diasporas and their ability to sustain themselves. He compares the diasporic Indian to a banyan tree:

> ...like the banyan tree, the traditional symbol of Indian way of life, he spreads out his roots in several soils, drawing nourishment from one when the rest dry up. Far from being homeless, he has several homes, and that is the only way he has increasingly come to feel at home in the world.[28]

While this particular capacity may be an excellent strategy for survival, it results in a life that is lived only on the surface. This is what creates the diasporic chasm in the sensibilities of people. In the case of the earliest Indian diasporas created out of indentures, it was not a spontaneous spreading out of roots but the painful growth of a support system for survival.

Outside the constricting realm of the Diaspora of indenture, there is another kind of Indian diaspora, which is mainly a twentieth century, post-independence phenomenon. The diasporic Indians belonging to this category are highly qualified professionals whose ambition takes them to other countries. They stay away from India for professional fulfilment and in most cases they settle abroad. This is the modern Indian diaspora, which is born out of self-choice. Identities are not beaten into shape, plurality is accepted as a natural consequence of one's choice:

> My self-description as an American is a spatial identity; constructed from the external territory, it has nothing to do with my *whatness*, my essence or *being* as a person, until the larger dominant culture readjusts itself to accommodate my presence...the territorial persona, as a mask of my identity, cannot fully represent the subject/object of my person, the material body and the psychic being.[29]

The dismantling of the cultural discourses of imperialism has ushered in diasporic writing and cultural theory in a big way in the literary arena but the inherent difference of forced choice and self-choice continues to manifest itself. An interesting example of this difference emerges in the manner in which Salman Rushdie and Amitav Ghosh look at diasporic Indians. Rushdie writes of displacement and loss:

> ...exiles or immigrants or expatriates are haunted by some sense of loss, some urge to reclaim, to look back, even at the risk of being mutated into pillars of salt. But if we do look back, we must do in knowledge—which gives rise to profound uncertainties—that our physical alienation from India almost inevitably means that we will not be capable of reclaiming precisely the thing that was lost; that we will, in short, create fictions, not actual cities or villages, but invisible ones, imaginary homelands, Indias of the mind.[30]

This stands in contrast with Amitav Ghosh's description of the Indian diaspora as a force to reckon with:

> The modern Indian diaspora...now represents an important force in world culture...the diaspora also counts among its members some of the finest writers: to my mind there are no finer writers writing in the English language today than V.S. Naipaul, Salman Rushdie and A.K. Ramanujan. In its own way the literary culture of the diaspora is also an important social and political—and, of course, literary-force within India.[31]

The Pulitzer Prize winning *Interpreter of Maladies* by Jhumpa Lahiri and *The Death of Vishnu*, a novel written by Manil Suri—an Indian professor of Mathematics in the U.S., substantiate Ghosh's claims. The process of Indian diasporic writing in English began with V.S. Naipaul, Ruth Prawer Jhabvala and Anita Desai; it was accelerated by Salman Rushdie and continues through the present generation of writers who are not "diasporic" in the strict sense of the term but have chosen to live abroad. Naipaul is an Indian by origin, Jhabvala by marriage and Desai by birth. Naipaul discovered India during his long visits to the land of his ancestors; Jhabvala stayed in India for many years after marriage and later moved on to New York; Anita Desai was born in India and lived most of her life here before moving on. India figures prominently in their works. While Naipaul in his writings attempts to dig out the maladies that ail the civilizations of the world and their modern predicament, Jhabvala writes with "a measure of racial chauvinism, which no amount of altruism can dispel. It is assumed...that the West is in several respects more organized, more coherent, more logical and more rational than the East."[32] Her new collection of short stories, *East to Upper East* is written on the same lines. In sharp contrast, Desai writes with an insider's vision. Naipaul's Hindu origin, Jhabvala's Polish parentage of Jewish descent and Desai's German-Bengali parentage have in their own way coloured the lived-in experience of these writers. Double geographical displacement in the case of Salman Rushdie has brought out significant renderings of "home" and "exile."

Rushdie was born, brought up and educated in Bombay till he went to Britain for his education. His family's migration to Pakistan in 1964 added another layer to his alienation. Like Naipaul, he had chosen exile for economic-professional reasons; like Naipaul he is a critic of the modern civilization. An equally interesting parallel emerges between Naipaul's Mohun Biswas (*A House for Mr Biswas*) and Rushdie's Salim Sinai (*Midnight's Children*). Both were born at midnight, both were victims of circumstance, both saw themselves as isolated figures struggling for an identity, both are the narrators of their respective stories, both die at the end of the novel having laid bare the limitations of the societies that they were born into. But Mohun Biswas and Salim Sinai differ on one major ground—while Salim Sinai is essentially a political creation, Mohun Biswas is above politics, religion and even history. Although he is a victim of circumstance, he looks beyond these constricting barriers. The difference between Rushdie and Naipaul is the difference between Mohun Biswas and Salim Sinai. Rushdie and Naipaul both share a preoccupation with history. Naipaul looks into history as a part of his prognosis for the present-day circumstance and voices the need for a total acceptance of history, however shameful. This is the only way history can be got rid of, rectified. Rushdie on the other hand toys with the possible rejection of a shameful history: "What to retain, what to dump, how to hold on to what memory insists on relinquishing, how to deal with change."[33] Rushdie has no difficulty in distancing himself from his roots because he spent a very happy and secure childhood in India and experienced its reality. He can therefore easily accommodate the pain and squalor of India. In Naipaul, this aspect of India stirs up a kind of traumatized rage. Rage becomes his stance to cope with the reality of his being.

The younger generation of NRI writers does not have to deal with their situation in the manner of Rushdie and Naipaul and this is very much evident in their writings. Vikram Chandra, Agha Shahid Ali, Bharati Mukherjee, Shashi Tharoor, Rohinton Mistry, Amitav Ghosh, and Vikram Seth enjoy the best of both worlds and do not suffer identity-related spasms. Shashi Tharoor easily accepts the plural identity of Indians: "...the singular thing about India is that you can only speak of it in the plural."[34] Vikram Chandra does not recognize physical distance as an alienating factor. He feels that "love and patriotism shouldn't be measured in terms of miles."[35] Distance does not alienate but personal circumstance does. Bharati Mukherjee says that she has "by marrying an American... become a very different person,—which means...a very different writer."[36]

This is in sharp contrast to Naipaul's first reaction to India. He found the distance too large to be bridged. It took him twenty-seven years and three books to arrive at an understanding of India. From the examples of the Indian writers living abroad, it is amply clear that a writer's vision is shaped by his/her lived-in experience and the experience he/she has inherited. Therefore the details of Naipaul's personal and inherited circumstance, which went into his making as a writer have to be accounted for.

Vidiadhar Surajprasad Naipaul was born in 1932 in an Indian-style house that his maternal grandfather had built in Chaguanas. His maternal grandfather had come to Trinidad as an indentured labourer on a five-year contract. He stayed on, made a lot of money and built a large house in Chaguanas. However, in 1926, he returned to India taking with him another woman with the intention of settling down in his native village in eastern Uttar Pradesh. His own wife and children stayed back. Unfortunately, he passed away during the train journey from Calcutta and never saw his village. The woman with him reached his village and settled there. Naipaul has written about his meeting with her in *An Area of Darkness* as well as in *Finding the Centre.* He writes that "her India had remained intact; her world had remained whole; no other idea of reality had broken through. It was different for thousands of others."[37] And that was because she was accepted and absorbed into the community. But thousands of Indians desperate to return had to face a different fate. Facing all odds they managed to book a passage on the *Ganges* that was to repatriate them but all that they saw on reaching Calcutta were "hundreds of derelicts, previously repatriated, who wanted now to be taken back.... India for these people had been a dream of home, a dream of continuity after the illusion of Trinidad. All the India they had found was the area around the Calcutta docks" (*FC* 53).

To Naipaul and his family India was just a far off dream. He grew up knowing nothing about his father's family and very little about his mother's family. It was only in 1972 that he got a complete idea of his family history. Indians had started coming to Trinidad around 1845 to replace the labour lost by the abolition of slave trade. They came on a five-year contract at the end of which they were to be given either a piece of land on the island or a free passage to India. But these promises were seldom kept and most Indians found themselves homeless and penniless at the end of five years. His paternal grandfather had come to Trinidad as an infant in the arms of his mother who had accepted indenture around 1880. His grandfather was trained to be a Pundit through sustained efforts of his mother so as to follow the family tradition. However, his grandfather died young, leaving behind a penniless widow and three children. The bereaved family was to be sent to India, but just before the ship was to sail out, the youngest child refused to go and cleverly hid himself till his mother changed her mind about going back to India. This child was Naipaul's father, Seepersad Naipaul. They stayed on in Trinidad. The eldest child, a daughter, was sent to work in a relative's house and she never learnt how to read or write. The elder son was sent to work on the sugar estates for a meagre eight cents a day. The younger son, Naipaul's father was sent to stay with a wealthy maternal uncle so that he could be educated and trained to be a Pundit. He went to school in the mornings and worked hard in his uncle's shop at night and thus got his education. He later became a journalist with the *Trinidad Guardian*. With the realization that dawned on him with the discovery of his family history in 1972, Naipaul says, he "worked back to a proper wonder" at his father's achievement (58).

Naipaul's father strove hard for "the life of the mind—the writer's life" and gave his children a good education.[38] Naipaul studied at the prestigious Queen's Royal College in Port of Spain and then moved on to the University College, Oxford on a Trinidad Government Scholarship. Naipaul's elder sister Kamla studied in the Women's College at Banaras Hindu University, also on a scholarship. It was in the letters of Kamla written from Banaras that Naipaul had his first real glimpse of India. The first letter in *Letters Between a Father and Son* is from a seventeen-year-old Naipaul to Kamla who was then staying in Varanasi. He urges her to keep her eyes open "and let me know whether Beverly Nicholas is right.... He saw the filth; refused to mention the 'spiritualness' that impresses another kind of visitor" (*Letters* 5). He writes to her of his opinion of Nehru's autobiography and of Aldous Huxley. In a letter to Kamla written two months after the first one, Naipaul writes: "I want you to promise that you will write a book in diary form about your stay in India...study conditions; analyse the character. Don't be too bitter. Try to be humorous." In order to cheer up his unhappy sister, he jokes about a book that she can think of writing. He even gives it a title—"*My Passage to India: A Record of Six Unhappy Months* by Kamla Naipaul" (8). Kamla never wrote the book but fifteen years later in 1964, Naipaul wrote *An Area of Darkness.*

Naipaul had inherited his ambition to be a writer from his father Seepersad Naipaul. Seepersad Naipaul had struggled all his life between financial dependence on his wife's family and his admiration for the craft of writing which he felt would help him break free from the "constrictions of Chaguanas" and the chaos of his wife's joint family (*FC* 71). Naipaul in *Finding the Centre* has recorded a gift he received from his father when he was three years old. It was a decorated anthology of poetry on which his father had inscribed:

> To Vidyadhar, from his father. Today you have reached the span of 3 years, 10 months and 15 days. And I make this present to you with this counsel in addition. Live up to the estate of man, follow truth, be kind and gentle and trust God. (*FC* 72)

It was his gift of 'the word' to his son. Two years later, when Naipaul was six, their unit in the joint family moved to Port of Spain to stay with his father. It was then that father and son came closer. Naipaul was introduced to his father's "book case-and-desk" (31). It was the first piece of furniture that he could call his own. Naipaul would go through his father's papers with a mixed sense of awe and delight at seeing his father's name in print. It was during this time that his father read *Oliver Twist* and *David Copperfield* to him. This love for Dickens stayed with him. Decades later in his self-explorations in *The Enigma of Arrival* he wrote: "Very few had the universal child's eye of Dickens."[39] Naipaul records this period as the "serenest" in his life. However, it did not last long. At the end of two years, the family was forced to return to the disorder of the joint family of his maternal grandmother.

Naipaul grew up amidst disorder and chaos and came to hate it. More so, after the two years of ordered life in Port of Spain. It was because of this repulsion for disorder that the father and son came closer. There was no relief even when the family moved back to Port of Spain after a two-year stay at the cocoa estate. With an ever-increasing number of relatives flowing in, their living space was cramped. But even then "like a wild religious faith that hardens in adversity, this wish to be a writer...strengthened..." (*FC* 38). Naipaul's father involved him in the making of a story that he was writing during those days. He read out each new part to him, each new turn of events and Naipaul watched it grow. Apart from this, his father also read out his other stories to him. In 1946, when Naipaul was fourteen, Seepersad Naipaul bought his own house and the family was on its own once again.

The idea of being a writer, "a fantasy of nobility," made young Naipaul want to break away from his world—"his family and clan, city, colony..." (38). In 1949, Naipaul won a Trinidad government scholarship and in 1950, he left for University College, Oxford to study English. In one of his earliest letters to his sister Kamla he writes of his departure from Trinidad: "...and at about 12.50, V.S. Naipaul was cut off from all family ties" (*Letters* 12). But physical distancing from Trinidad was not enough. Naipaul felt weighed down by his closed upbringing, he could not relate to other societies: "My inability to understand other societies made nonsense of the Huxley and D.H. Lawrence and the Evelyn Waugh I tried to read..." (*FC* 39). Then there were the confusions of history. Naipaul had to grow up "with two ideas of history, almost two ideas of time" (51). One of these was the history he studied at school that was comprehensible and the other was the history of his ancestry that he came across at home. The latter seemed to him to be extremely remote and "almost as imaginary as the land of the *Ramayana*..." (52). Citing an example of the year 1919, Naipaul explains how 1919 as the year of Gandhi's first call for civil disobedience in India seemed recent but 1919 in the life of the Indians in Trinidad was "a time, beyond recall, mythical" (51). These confusions plagued him throughout. "True knowledge of geography and with it a sense of historical wonder" came to him many years later while he was working on a history of the Trinidad islands (42). He read about the region, about Sir Walter Ralegh's raids, like he had never read in a school textbook. He also discovered the original name and history of his birthplace, Chaguanas. In his pursuit of the profession of a writer, Naipaul wanted to cut himself off from his past. He hoped he would never have to "come back to Trinidad" (*Letters* 221), and if he did, he would "die from intellectual starvation" (298). But then, after writing his first book, Naipaul awoke to a new realization:

> To become a writer, that noble thing, I had thought it necessary to leave. Actually to write, it was necessary to go back. It was the beginning of self-knowledge. (*FC* 40)

In *The Enigma of Arrival,* Naipaul has described his earliest attempts at being a writer. He has described how at the age of eighteen he had written a short piece called 'The Gala Night' based on metropolitan material. The "fracture" between the writing and the man that he described, surfaced many a time:

> ...the idea given me by my education...was that the writer was a person possessed of sensibility; that the writer was someone who recorded or displayed an inward development. So...the ideas of Bloomsbury, ideas bred essentially out of empire, wealth and imperial security had been transmitted to me in Trinidad. To be that kind of writer (as I interpreted it) I had to be false; I had to pretend to be other than I was, other than what a man of my background could be. Concealing this colonial-Hindu self below the writing personality, I did both my material and myself much damage. (*EOA* 134)

The man and the writer that had separated in 1950 on leaving Trinidad came together five years later in 1955 in a BBC room in London as the typewriter clicked away a distant Port of Spain memory: "*Every morning when he got up Hat would sit on the banister of his back verandah and shout across, 'What happening there, Bogart?*'" (*FC* 16). There was no looking back after that. Books followed in quick succession amidst widespread acclaim. The writer had been made, the father's dream accomplished.

The very fact that Naipaul had to turn to his "colonial-Hindu" self for his material implies directly that his writing would be built around his diasporic concerns. *The Mystic Masseur* (1957), *The Suffrage of Elvira* (1958) and *Miguel Street* (1959), his first three books span the period from the beginning of World War II to around 1950. All three are genial satires on the Trinidad society. *Miguel Street* (1959), a collection of seventeen stories, is a record of the observations of the author. The language is the original Trinidadian English. It is written with a concern but with a certain detachment too. In the end the narrator leaves the street and goes to England for an education because he "...no longer wanted to be like Eddoes."[40] It is the first record of his insights as a Trinidad East Indian. The *Mystic Masseur* (1957) sees the rise of Ganesh (a carryover from Ganesh Pundit) from a nonentity to G. Ramsay Muir, Esq., M.B.E. It is a rise from failure to success. *The Suffrage of Elvira* (1958) is about democracy coming to an obscure island of multi-ethnic population. On the surface, these three books are comical renditions but the undercurrent of pathos and satire is equally strong.

If his first three books were about the perplexities of various rootless individuals and their efforts to make a mark on their host society, his next book is an examination of the same theme in a more elaborate manner. The comic is replaced by pathos: there is a single protagonist, a Trinidad East Indian, striving to follow the profession of his Pundit ancestors in India. He wants to be a scholar (Pundit) and writer, and in order to be so he has to struggle against conflicting inputs from within and without. It is also a record of the life of three generations of Indians in Trinidad—the diaspora's development and the deracinating effect that grows stronger as years pass. *A House for Mr. Biswas* (1961) is thus Naipaul's first full-fledged account of the Indian diaspora in Trinidad. And it is from here that all his subsequent diasporic concerns can be traced.

In 1962, Naipaul travelled to India and during his stay here, he wrote his only novel with English characters and English setting, *Mr. Stone and the Knights Companion* (1963). 1962 also saw the publication of *The Middle Passage* a non-fiction work on the Caribbean for which the Government of Trinidad officially commissioned him. This book aroused instant and intense criticism and Naipaul was accused of criticizing the West Indian populace. The book declared that the middle passage—the deportation of millions from Africa to the New World as slaves had not been blocked; this passage continued on renewed patterns of mass emigration and thrived on the slavish mentality of the West Indians. However, *A House for Mr. Biswas* marks a sharp change from the bitter criticism of his earlier works. In 1962 he travelled to India, to the land of his ancestors. He intended to write a novel on India but abandoned the idea. *An Area of Darkness* (1964) on the surface seems to be the work of an irritable and unsympathetic traveller. But then, the see-saw of the love-hate relationship of what he saw against what he had imagined cannot be denied. The area of darkness spread, and this first dark vision of India found its development in *The Mimic Men* (1967). *The Mimic Men* takes on the topic of the predicament of the Trinidad East-Indian society under the overriding influences of the western world. The pathos in *A House for Mr. Biswas* is replaced by despair in *The Mimic Men.* It is the despair of an emigrant student, the social problems of the West Indian society, the despair of a colony struggling for an identity and the predicament of unending mimicry. Naipaul speaks "discursively on politics, power, isolation, displacement, racial conflicts and identity. He examines the educational system of the colonies, which, with its accent on things irrelevant to the local situation, produces mimic men."[41] This idea found expression in *India: A Wounded Civilization* (1997) in which Naipaul tried to get to the root of the maladies ailing India.

Naipaul's works of fiction and non-fiction are closely related. All the while, in all his writing, he is working on the problems and after-effects of the socio-geographical displacements during the colonial rule that later reduced independence to a mere act of mimicry. *The Loss of El Dorado* (1969), deeply steeped in historical research, explores the motives and realities of Ralegh's raid on the inviolate world of the mythical Golden City of El Dorado. It not only works back at history but also looks forward and explains why the transition from the past to the present cannot be a smooth one, why the present is still shackled to the past, why it is yet to be created. In 1971, the Booker Prize winning *In A Free State* came as "a rather final statement" of the themes running through his first phase of fiction writing.[42] It captures the feeling of being in a void, incapable of any positive action. Naipaul then turned to alternative modes of narrative to accommodate his ever-growing social and political concerns. In the three decades that followed, Naipaul moved towards non-fiction.

After reading *The Mimic Men,* Alastair Niven had wondered if Naipaul could write another novel.[43] Although *In A Free State* (1971) proved Niven wrong, but its mixture of fiction and non-fiction in a way vindicated Niven's stand. The next three decades witnessed the Naipaulian shift from fiction to non-fiction. Of the thirteen books that Naipaul came out with between 1972-1999, seven were works of non-fiction, two were classified as autobiography, and four were works of fiction. *An Overcrowded Barracoon* (1972) is a collection of essays divided into three sections. The first section deals with Naipaul's world as colonial and its implications in the world of Naipaul the writer. The second section contains Naipaul's views on India and the third section crystallizes Naipaul's vision and interpretation of the failure of former colonies to break away from a repetitive performance of the patterns of the "civilized" and the "primitive." Naipaul has drawn dismal pen portraits of the island countries in search of nationhood, and of the permanent damage caused by colonial rule. *Guerrillas* (1975) and *A Bend in the River* (1979) are both fictionalized versions of actual political occurrences and record the final collapse of an already debilitated social order. *India: A Wounded Civilization* (1977), his second book on India, sees it as a civilization repeatedly attacked by foreign forces, saddled with imported institutions that make a mockery of its independence. *The*

Return of Eva Peron with the Killings in Trinidad (1980) is a collection of four essays that forwards Naipaul's thesis of the cruelty of the sixteenth-century being perpetrated even at the end of the twentieth century. *Among the Believers* (1981) presents Naipaul's observation of the societies of Iran, Pakistan, Malaysia and Indonesia. He investigates the political power that Islam had come to wield in the twentieth century and in *Beyond Belief: Islamic Excursions Among the Converted Peoples* (1998) he continues with his exploration of these four non-Arab Islamic countries. He sees non-Arab Muslims as peoples whose racial culture stands contested by their religious faith and in the confusion that follows people lose sight of themselves and forget who they are. *A Turn in the South* (1989) is a record of his observations of societies as diverse as Atlanta and rural Mississippi. *Finding the Centre* (1984) is Naipaul's autobiographical attempt to trace his "literary beginnings and the imaginative promptings" of his "many-sided background" (*FC* 9). This process of the making of the writer is further analysed in *The Enigma of Arrival* (1987). Although it is classified as fiction, this book is an in-depth self-exploration of Naipaul's early years as a writer and his grappling with the question of identify. As he concludes, Naipaul writes that it was during the "Hindu Death Ceremony" of his sister that he came to accept that "Men need history" in order "to have an idea of who they are" and this idea is remade by every passing generation (*EOA* 318). However obscure this sacred idea might be, it is indispensable. *India: A Million Mutinies Now* (1990), Naipaul's third book on India, is different from his other two books on India. It is a kind of final homecoming for Naipaul because he could now see India being "restored to itself."[44] The book is as much about Naipaul as it is about India. Naipaul had steadily progressed towards a vision of terrible loss and eternal mimicry as the modern predicament of the third world societies. *The Enigma of Arrival* had marked a change in this vision and *India: A Million Mutinies Now* changed it completely. *A Way In The World* (1994) comprises of nine narratives in which Naipaul goes back to his theses of *The Middle Passage, The Loss of El Dorado, In a Free State,* and *Finding the Centre* in a more expansive vision.

Naipaul's literary career is a bold attempt at an honest portrayal of his view of the world that he inhabits. His vision has grown and changed over a period of time and he belongs to that rare variety of writers who have no qualms about going back and correcting themselves. He accepts the limitations of his experience:

> And how could my knowledge of the world not be abstract, when all the world I knew at the age of eighteen was the small colonial world of my little island...our little Asian Indian community: Small world within small world. (*EOA* 130)

He discloses that his initial denial of his experience was a blunder:

> Thinking of myself as a writer, I was hiding my experience from myself; hiding myself from my experience. And even when I became a writer I was without the means, for many years, to cope with that disturbance. (117)

Naipaul has continuously defined himself through his writing; through his writing he discovered the worlds that he contained within himself; he realized that his subject was not his "sensibility" but the different worlds that he "lived in" (135). He writes: "To get anywhere in the writing I had first of all to define myself very clearly to myself" (145). Naipaul's engagement with India falls within this framework. His idea of India was not his own. It had been handed down to him by his family. This idea of India was a part of his idea of himself, which too was initially an inheritance. It was a world which he carried within him. When faced with the real India, he felt the India within him falling apart, and the man and the writer had to come to terms with it. The unity of his world was lost forever and the writing had to begin from an impossible place: a place of an un-healing wound, a place of immense loss and pain, a place where a highly charged memory is placed under erasure.

2

BROKEN DREAMS

> Hysteria had been my reaction, and a brutality dictated by a new awareness of myself as a whole human being and a determination, touched with fear, to remain what I was.
>
> V.S. Naipaul, *An Area of Darkness.*

India shocked Naipaul because it challenged his idea of himself. The contradiction between the imagined India of Trinidad and the actual country was too overwhelming to be confronted. The only immediate solution available was that of escape. That is why *An Area of Darkness* begins with 'A Resting Place for the Imagination' and ends in 'Flight'—a metaphoric fleeing away from his reality. But the experience of India does not end with the crossing over of its geo-political boundaries. In far off Madrid, with India twenty-four hours behind him, Naipaul reflects: "It was a journey that ought not to have been made; it had broken my life in two" (*AD* 265). This chapter focuses on the latter half of the statement and sees in it an explanation for the first half. It attempts to read *An Area of Darkness* as the first phase of a diasporic writer's engagement with the land of his origin; a phase that must essentially begin with an 'imagined' idea of the land. Although the chapter discusses the body of criticism that followed the publication of *An Area of Darkness*, specially in India, the stress is not on the truth/bias of Naipaul's vision. The chapter presents an exposition of the first phase in a diasporic writer's imagination and an assimilation and explanation of the process of his coming to terms with his diasporic status.

Naipaul's idea of India found its way to him through the very fact of his birth into a Hindu joint family in Trinidad. India lay around him "in people" and "in things" ever since he gained consciousness. One of his earliest memories is of Gold Teeth Nanee and her grave dignified husband whose fierce loyalty to their language (they spoke only Hindi) and to the Indian way of life made them look like foreigners in Trinidad. They carried their India within them. It was not fragmented by their Trinidadian reality, which they "denied" by their refusal to recognize it. India also existed around Naipaul in the various domestic articles that his grandfather had brought from India:

> India lay about us in things: in a string bed...in plaited straw mats; in innumerable brass vessels;...in brightly coloured pictures of deities on pink lotus or radiant against Himalayan snow; and in all the paraphernalia of the prayer-room...the images, the smooth pebbles, the stick of sandalwood. (29)

Although he lived within the India created by his grandfather, he could not inherit the unity of his grandfather's world. His grandfather had "carried his village with him" and in his re-creation of this village he had "denied" Trinidad completely (30). Therefore, his world remained whole. Naipaul's generation could not replicate that sense of complete self-sufficiency; it could not "deny Trinidad." As he grew, India slipped further and further away. It belonged to his grandfather's world, a world which the younger generations had no access to. The rituals and ceremonies of their private world survived but the corresponding knowledge was lost: "our elders expected that our understanding would be instinctive—and no one explained the prayer or ritual" (32). All of Hinduism that remained with him was a "sense of the difference of people...a vaguer sense of caste, and a horror of the unclean" (32-33). These three ideas manifest themselves repeatedly throughout *An Area of Darkness.* Another introduction to the Indian way of life was through the stories that his father wrote:

> These stories celebrated Indian village life, and the Hindu rituals that gave grace and completeness to that life...to

> me they gave a beauty...to the Indian village life I had never known. And when we went to the country to visit my father's own relations,...it was like a fairytale come to life. (*FC* 36)

Following the same analogy, Naipaul expected India to be a land of his fairytale. His communication with his sister Kamla (who studied in India) ought to have prepared him for disillusionment but strangely, it did not. In the first chapter of *An Area of Darkness*, 'A Resting-Place for the Imagination,' two distinct personas of Naipaul emerge. One is the persona of a totally self-aware non-believer with an actual distaste for rituals. The other is the one who is outraged to hear that candles and electric bulbs had replaced clay lamps for Diwali in Bombay; who quietly backs out of a science experiment at school that required him to suck from a common siphon; who could be angered by Beverly Nicholas's *Verdict on India*. These two separate selves had stayed together as long as Naipaul was in Trinidad or in England. There was a public life and a private family life. The direct experience of India tore these two selves apart; his life was broken into two. *An Area of Darkness* is a portrayal of the friction between the two selves. To say that *An Area of Darkness* is about India, is to miss the point altogether. It is a desperate attempt to preserve the unity of a sensibility shattered beyond repair. The method employed is one of dismissal, rejection and flight. The realization of the inefficacy of this method produced *India: A Million Mutinies Now*. The 'Flight' marked the beginning of a series of journeys to India.

An Area of Darkness is divided into three parts and eleven sub-parts. It also has a prologue—'Traveller's Prelude: A Little Paperwork' and an epilogue—'Flight.' The sub-parts are closely linked patterns of his experiences and their examinations. 'A Resting Place for the Imagination' provides the background for Naipaul's understanding of India. 'Degree,' 'The Romancers' and 'The Colonial' are three major aspects of India that he encounters. 'Degree' for Naipaul stands as an Indian's understanding of himself. String-cots and wooden blocks had lain unused in his Trinidad home for the lack of people of that "caste skill" (*AD* 29). But that was not so in India. People had accepted work outside the realm of their "caste-skill" and in doing so, they had not forgotten their "degree." This double realization, instead of protecting the unity of his world, worked in a paradoxical manner and led to a split at a very interior level in his Indian psyche. This "knowledge of degree" which Naipaul finds "in the bones" of Indians makes it difficult for them to combat the social confusion and disorder of castes (55). Ramnath, the steno, refused to type because that was not *his* job. Malhotra with an English university education does not recognize such job divisions. Ramnath's humiliation arises not so much out of his submission to Malhotra as out of the violation of his "degree": he, a steno, had been made to do a typist's job. Another example of keeping of "degree" is Jivan. Jivan rose from an odd-job boy in a printery to an office clerk with a side business that earned him as much money as the English university educated Malhotra but Jivan continued to sleep on pavements. Vasant began as a telegram agent and became an established stockbroker, but he kept his habit of skipping lunch—a habit that belonged to his days of austerity. The two Brahmin brothers in the south had risked their caste and started a leather business but were "anxious to protect their children against caste contamination" (55). Naipaul finds the incongruities of the "imported mechanics of the new world" being "incorporated into the rule of degree" (56). People like Malik and Malhotra who did not recognize this "degree" were exceptional and their rejection of "degree" left them rejected. Then there is the Bunty, Andy brand of Indian who sleepwalks through life and delights in its "new closeness to power" (60). It is this category of sleepwalkers that Naipaul wants to "shake" up by "the shoulder" (60-61). Their static nature, their inability to respond to their situation leaves Naipaul puzzled. The chapter ends with an analysis of Manohar Malgonkar's *The Prince* and an acceptance of "degree" which is at once, an Indian typicality as well as a typically Indian confusion, that an outsider has to deal with.

'The Colonial' is a chapter which takes up another view of post-independence India. It records the split in the eastern and the western mindset through the example of beggary in India. Naipaul notes that a foreigner cannot understand "the function of the beggar in India" which makes the act of charity an "automatic reverence to God, like the offering of a candle or a spin of the prayer-wheel" (68-69). Naipaul records the phenomenon of Indian defecation in great detail and this part of *An Area of Darkness* had earned him scathing criticism from India. However, this is not a mere chronicling of fact. Naipaul attempts an analysis. Defecation is unrepresented in novels, stories, films and in documentaries not because of a "prettifying intention" on the part of the people of India but because *"Indians do not see these squatters."* Naipaul calls it "a collective blindness" that arises out of "the Indian fear of pollution" (70). Indians refuse to *see* the existence of dirt. This is followed by Naipaul's much-disputed hypothesis on Gandhi. It was Gandhi's "colonial" vision and his critical "South African eye" that made him look at India "as no Indian" was able to (73). Sanitation in India was linked to caste-designated roles and a break up of the caste system had filled the country with filth. Gandhi *saw* the maladies of India, he tried to *dignify* labour, and he tried to *delink* the caste moulds from a man's function in society. He united a diverse nation as no one else could have done. But in the end, he himself was absorbed into the great Indian symbolism. He was deified but his message was lost. The India that he sought to change placed him on a pedestal and continued on its own way.

'Romancers' is about the dilution of the real to create the imaginary. Mrs. Mahindra with her "craze for foreign" and Mrs. M. Mehta, Secretary of Women's League, attempt to escape from their traditional roles. There is new money and the freedom that it brings. Naipaul is sympathetic towards the plight of Mrs. Mahindra but he is critical of her response to her situation which, to use a favourite Naipaulian word is only a "mimicry," a misplaced sense of romance. He sees it as a malaise that arises out of an individual's absence of a sure sense of self and as a poor substitute to fill up the gaps in one's cultural make-up. Naipaul could not share the romance of the Indian films or of the *shikara* boats because he was neither "English" nor "Indian;" he was "denied the victories of both" (98). With this painful realization the first part of *An Area of Darkness* comes to an end. The first part is the body from which Naipaul's responses in the second part and the third part of the book are derived. It marks the first phase in Naipaul's search for a response to India. The result of this search was the discovery of his being an outsider to the realm of responses that could only be either English or Indian.

The second part, which comprises of three chapters, is an exploration. Naipaul offered himself to the experience of India. This part is filled with conversations through which Naipaul attempts to carve out a picture of India. 'A Doll's House on Dal Lake' is the make-believe world of Mr. Butt, Aziz and the *khansamah*: "Snow White's own men" trying to survive long after 'Snow White' had left (140). These men have no idea of themselves. They continually seek to make commercial benefits. Their concern, hospitality and friendliness have theatrical dimensions. They all want typewritten certificates from Naipaul because they think that these would add to their credibility. Aziz is an expert in the art of pleasing. His foil is the *khansamah* who has never learnt the art and as a result remains a tormented man. Naipaul's interactions with the *khansamah* bring out a fine analysis of anger. The *khansamah's* anger and the almost simultaneous "recognition of his own weakness" made him a "tormented man." Naipaul felt himself to be as inadequate as the *khansamah*:

> I suffered with him...and I was surprised by the rise within myself of that deep anger which unhinges judgment and almost physically limits vision...the moment of anger is a moment of exhalted, shrinking lucidity from which recovery is slow and shattering. (117)

Naipaul observed that with the going of imperial rule, "one type of glory had gone" and the "other type hadn't set in" (119). It was a period of blankness lived in the shadow of the past. "English taste" was flaunted as "superior" and Indian taste was "inferior" (119). Naipaul, the foreign man could issue coveted certificates from his typewriter, he could be used to obtain a tourist permit from the "Touriasm" (117). Amidst all this were also orthodox Hindu pilgrims who, like the Trinidad Indians, carried their world with them and "denied" everything else. Even while they stayed at Liward and cooked and washed on its lawn, Mr. Butt, Aziz and the *khansamah* remained beyond their "pure" existence. And with the departure of the *khansamah* Naipaul says "the vision of the hotel as doll's house altered" (117).

The 'Medieval City,' on the surface, deals with the features of Srinagar. Naipaul sees people who have forgotten their history and survive on legend. That is how Akbar's "late sixteenth century fort in the Dal Lake" came to be regarded as five thousand years old (125). The details of "the man" who had brought the Hazratbal relic were not known; "Religion...was life and the Law..." (128). The Muslim medical student did not believe that the world was made in six days but "was more of a religious fanatic than Aziz who, secure in his system inspected other systems with tolerant interest..." (129). Naipaul studies the "medieval mind" which could "casually" assess a building as five thousand years old (129). This same capacity facilitated other amnesias. The medieval mind could easily forget the last three to four hundred years of its past:

> And it was because it was without a sense of history that it was capable of so complete a conversion. Many Kashmiri clan names—like that of Mr. Butt himself—were often still purely Hindu; but of their Hindu past the Kashmiris retained no memory. (129)

Naipaul finds the Valley suffering from selective amnesia. The engineer who was showing the valley to Naipaul, drove past the eighth century Awantipur ruins and showed no interest in them. Naipaul observed that the history of the people in the valley began with the history of their conquerors. Amidst the common populace, Sheikh Abdullah had already passed into legend. Their accounts of 1947 "ignored Congress, Gandhi, British, the Pakistan invasion" (131). Naipaul was battling to break out of the visitor mode and a chance encounter with a family on his way back from Awantipur helped him to connect:

> In India I had so far felt myself a visitor. Its size, its temperatures, its crowds: I had prepared myself for these, but in its very extremes, the country was alien.

> Looking for the familiar, I had again, in spite of myself, become an islander: I was looking for the small and manageable. (140)

His encounter with the family, its observance of food related rules, the power patterns in the family all at once evoked a Port of Spain memory and Naipaul found that the gap of three generations and of a lost language had been bridged. For a fleeting second he was able to relate to his experience of India.

'Pilgrimage' begins with a description of the five-foot ice *lingam* of Amarnath:

> It was a mystery, like Delphi, of the older world. It had survived because it was of India and Hinduism which, without beginning, without end, scarcely a religion, continued as a repository and living record of man's religious consciousness. (154)

The chapter is an account of Naipaul's journey to the Amarnath cave, his encounter with Laraine—'the seeker,' and a brief interlude of the missing *ghora-wallah*. The chapter also witnesses Naipaul's encounter with the 'Himalayas' of his Trinidadian childhood (167). Passing through the complicated finances of travel with Aziz and the trickery of the *ghora-wallah*, Naipaul met Laraine, who was "attracted to Hindu philosophy" and had decided to join an ashram (162). The poor sense of sanitation on the part of the *yatris* had irked Naipaul but Laraine scarcely noticed this. She floated from one illusion to another. First she wanted to join an ashram and learn Hindu philosophy. Then she converted to Islam and married the Muslim sitarist Rafiqu. Very soon, she deserted him and went to an ashram and later left the country. The 'seeker' had been torn apart by her illusions. The reality always managed to elude her.

Himalayas, the next prominent feature of the chapter had a special place in Naipaul's childhood memory:

> I felt linked to them...India, the Himalayas: they went together. In so many of the brightly coloured religious

> pictures in my grandmother's house I had seen these mountains, cones of white against simple, cold blue. They had become a part of the India of my fantasy. (167)

But when he encountered the actual Himalayas, they seemed to him "as the Indian symbol of loss" (167). They were at once near and far: near in the imagination but almost inaccessible to the vast populace which could seek them only in "pilgrimages, legends and pictures?" (167). Naipaul reveals that he knew that there was no truth in the pictures of Himalayas which he had seen in Trinidad but in spite of this knowledge a part of his mind continued to believe in the possibility of the pictures' truth. 'Pilgrimage' thus establishes that India for Naipaul is something which cannot be claimed. What he says of the Himalayas is also true for his own experience. He can only look back at India "with yearning;" he can only return to it "in pilgrimages, legends and pictures?" (167). It is on this note that the second part of the book ends.

The third part begins with 'Fantasy and Ruins.' It is Naipaul's direct confrontation with his imagination. He digs up the roots of his imagination and dissects his past experiences: his experiences as a colonial in Trinidad, his experience of England as it existed in Trinidad; his experience of Kipling and other writers on India; and of his idea of India that he had formed in Trinidad. He was unprepared to accept the England that he saw in India:

> This confirmation laid bare a small area of self-deception which, below knowledge and self-knowledge, had survived in that part of my mind which held as a possibility the existence of the white Himalayan cones against a cold blue sky, as in the religious pictures in my grandmother's house. For in the India of my childhood, the land which in my imagination was an extension, separate from the alienness by which we ourselves were surrounded, of my grandmother's house, there was no alien presence. (187)

Naipaul looks into himself and wonders why the "detachment" he had cultivated during the prolonged isolations of his stay in England, deserted him in India. He sees in India's acceptance of England, the typical Indian ability "to retreat, the ability genuinely not to see what was obvious" (188). Ironically, this is what kept India whole. Naipaul saw that this ability "to retreat," first lead to "passivity," then to "detachment" and finally to "acceptance" (188). He realizes that he had been very close to this pattern of survival during his stay in England. But then, nothing could prepare him for the experience of India. Of the reminders of England in India, he writes:

> I ought to have been calm. But they revealed one type of self-deception as self-deception; and though this was lodged in that part of the mind where fantasy was permissible, the revelation was painful. It was an encounter with a humiliation I had never before experienced, and perhaps more so to me than to those Indians who hurried about streets with unlikely English names.... (188)

He compares and contrasts the British Empires in the West Indies and in India in an attempt to account for the difference in his response to the England that he saw in India. He sees India living with the Raj that was long dead. India thus becomes for Naipaul a country that lived amongst incongruous, "alien ruins" (190) because in India "every thing is inherited, nothing is abolished" (194).

From here he moves on to a detailed analysis of literature and its chronicling of the societies of its times. He finds that British 'British' is very different from the imperial Indian usage of the term (195-201). The latter is a creation of fantasy. It is a concept of "Englishness" that has outlived the Empire. In India, it exists in unending mimicry of the Raj. The Raj itself being a classical case of imitation of all that was thought to be "English," the inheritors of the Raj followed the same pattern. India goes on living with the ruins of the Empire. There are other kinds of ruins that lie across the length and breadth of the country: the ruins of Vijaynagar, the ravages of Muslim rule in the North, and the disjointed idea of history in the minds of the people. The creation in India is built on destruction. There is no continuity and plunder is the main predecessor of creation. With the coming of the British, this discontinuity became most prominent. Art sought to imitate.

The Raj sought to express "an idea" of itself as "English." Nationalist India accepted this as an established pattern. It too sought to express "an idea" of itself (207). In the process art was lost. Naipaul cites the example of the Indian memorial of the Mutiny at Lucknow and of the new temple at Kurukshetra. The beauty, the originality of art was lost, "Somewhere something has snapped," says Naipaul (207). The British were responsible for the death of Indian art, for the break in continuity. "A biscuit factory can hardly be a substitute for pearl trade and gold embroidery" (208).

Hindu India had faced other conquerors in the past but they had been absorbed into the mainstream. "Hindu India met conquerors half-way and had always been able to absorb them" (209). This continuity was broken with the coming of the British:

> The British refused to be absorbed into India; they did not proclaim, like the Mogul, that if there was a paradise on earth, it was this, and it was this, and it was this. While dominating India they expressed their contempt for it, and projected England; and Indians were forced into a nationalism.... It was an immense self-violation;...a flattering self-assessment could only be achieved with the help of Europeans like Max Muller.... (211)

The rejection of India and the projection of England created chaos. Indians found themselves "in a new world whose forms they could see but whose spirit eluded them. In the acquiring of an identity in their own land they became displaced" (212). Naipaul cites a moving example of the damage done to India's idea of itself. Newspaper items on India were short statements of facts because they were 'Indian' and hence unimportant. Whereas a newspaper item relating to far off Belgium was "big news" and required to be reported in detail (213). The incongruity was everywhere. It was routinely carried out in courts whose proceedings and language were foreign to the people involved. Unlike other languages bequeathed to India by its conquerors, English never became an Indian language. It remained a foreign language and paradoxically, it continued to be used. "Language is like a sense" says Naipaul, and "the psychological damage caused by the continued official use of English...is immense" (213). He found that the creative use of English was also deficient and translations could "never do justice to the Indian 'language' writers" (215). English could never be the medium of expression of Indian sentiments. It took away the proximity of emotions that the process of reading generates and presented a superficial tabulation of Indian sentimentality. Premchand in translation lost his edge.

Throughout the chapter Naipaul has steadily worked towards laying bare the ultimate damage caused to the Indian psyche during the colonial rule. He explains that "Indian sentimentality" is India's way of turning away, of diluting the pain of its reality. It is the use of selective amnesia to preserve an idea of unity that no longer exists. It is India's defence mechanism:

> It is well that Indians are unable to look at their country directly, for the distress they would see would drive them mad...which Indian would be able to read the history of his country for the last thousand years without anger and pain? It is better to retreat into fantasy and fatalism.... (210)

It is this defence mechanism at work that he finds in R.K. Narayan's novels. One needs 'Indian' eyes to be able to see Narayan's world. Naipaul writes that Narayan's vision is rooted; it has that inimitable synthesis of concern and total acceptance of the predicament of India (216). Naipaul finds this missing in the younger generation of writers in English. In Ruth Prawer Jhabvala's novels he finds "an acceptable type of comment" because her vision is not rooted (216). For Naipaul, it is not the question of the validity of Jhabvala's vision or the validity of Narayan's vision. It is a question of the difference in experience that creates difference in vision. In this chapter, Naipaul comes up with a Gordian knot. He finds India to be a victim of its capacity to endure, of its acceptance of everything in order to maintain a sense of continuity which in reality, is just an illusion. On the other hand, he finds that India survived the colonial experience only on account of its ability to accept its predicament as an unexamined continuity. The contradiction is fatal. It froze India and made it static. None of the conquerors before the coming of the British had forced India into such a sterile state. Independent India moved on the same pattern of non-existent continuity. "Englishness" was still affected in higher social circles. The common Indian still listened to the proceedings in courts being conducted in English in independent India with the same bewilderment as he had done during imperial rule. The sterility was total. "Shiva has ceased to dance," says Naipaul (217). This false sense of continuity needs to be broken if India is to go on.

In the next chapter, 'The Garland on my Pillow' Naipaul records his meetings with various people. The picture that emerges is that of an India in conflict. It is a conflict that arises out of ignorance. An Inspector of Forms and Stationery in the Northern Railway is non-existent for a Railway officer busy with his "presidential tours" (220). The cigarette smoking Sikh has a violent hatred for Dravidians. He is proud of his Aryan lineage and regards non-Aryans with contempt. He is vociferous in his impatience with India. The figure of the Sikh at the beginning of the chapter seems to emerge as an extension of Naipaul's response to the pain, squalor and poverty of India. Naipaul shuns the hospitality of the sweetshop-owner and prefers the company of the Sikh. But later, Naipaul is able to see the difference in the Sikh's debunking of India and the painful hysteria of his own response. While the Sikh was responding to an "idea" of himself, Naipaul saw himself responding to India with a "Love insensibly turned into a self-lacerating hysteria..." (230). The Sikh's hatred was venomous. It was without concern. Naipaul was able to detach himself from the Sikh's reactions: "He was reacting for me, as he had done on the train. But now I knew my hysteria for what it was. The words were his, not mine. They broke the spell" (230).

Leaving the Sikh, Naipaul went to the sweetshop-owner and let himself be overtaken by his hospitality. He was grateful for the warmth and kindness of India. He wanted it to remain as such. He feared that this softness and warmth could be lost in the violence of our times. In the end he returns to his hotel room to find a typically Indian show of appreciation by one of his readers. His room was filled with incense smoke, there were flowers strewn all over his bed and there was a garland on his pillow. The incense suffocated him, his eyes watered on account of the smoke, his room was littered with ash, but still, this was an appreciation that touched his heart. It was genuine. It soothed the rawness of his self-inflicted hysteria. It was India's way of reaching out.

The next chapter 'Emergency' presents Indian responses to the Chinese attack on India. The attack had caught India unawares and the Emergency only meant more speeches, more statutes of law. The common man and the politician both were feeding on words. The elite casually discussed the war as if it were something totally remote from them and calmly returned to the routine of their dinners and discussions. The lectures at the Theosophical Society were monotonous and irrelevant to the situation at hand. He saw the Aurobindo Society in Pondicherry as a "self-contained organization, efficiently run by its members" (240). Here too, the world centred around Sri Aurobindo, and after him, around The Mother. As is bound to happen with mono-centric organizations, the loss of the centre spells chaos. In Calcutta, Naipaul tries to find the city that had been the cradle of Indian renaissance. He found the "products of the dead Indian renaissance" to whom, Independence was merely an opportunity to withdraw from India, to step into the show of being "British" (245). Durgapur, the steel town was a small point of hope for revival. No sooner had Naipaul crossed Durgapur, he was beset with doubt. The survival of this small point of hope looked threatened with the news of the defeat of the Indian Army on the Indo-Chinese border. Nehru's speeches were already beginning to sound like "helpless condolence" (245).

The chapter also describes an Indian commissioner's absurd obsession with soaps and shoes. The people belonging to the area under his charge made shoes and soaps. But the story behind his obsession with soaps and shoes is a moving one. It was his defence, for himself and for his daughter, who in far off England was deeply distressed when she had heard that "no one wore shoes" or "washed" in India (247). Beneath this soap and shoe display Naipaul sees the hands of craftsmen and is comforted by the thought that "with so little encouragement and such poor materials" these people were still able to exercise their craftsmanship (247). In his speeches the commissioner exhorted the people to grow more food, to grow strong and skilled to fight the Chinese. However, very soon all these preparations of civil defence in towns and cities alike passed into routine and were lost. On a trip to Lucknow, Mr. Nehru lost his temper on seeing the civil defence practices. "All this digging of trenches, he said, was a waste of time" (251). And thus India returned to its routine existence. The Chinese attack and the emergency soon slipped into legend. In spite of everything, the experience of India that Naipaul had articulated in the previous chapter is seen progressing towards a greater acceptance in this chapter. He rejects his thesis of the Sikhs being the only "few whole men in India" (222). He now finds a different kind of value in Indians as human beings:

> Out of all its squalor and human decay, its eruptions of butchery, India produced so many people of grace and beauty, ruled by elaborate courtesy. Producing too much life, it denied the value of life; yet it permitted a unique human development to so many. Nowhere were people so heightened, rounded and individualistic; nowhere did, they offer themselves so fully and with such assurance. To know Indians was to take a delight in people as people.... I did not want India to sink; the mere thought was painful. (243)

The 'Village of the Dubes,' is the last chapter in the book. Naipaul records his visit to the ancestral village of his maternal grandfather. He was afraid of what he might find; he was afraid that the final unity of his world in his grandmother's house might be shattered. In the beginning he was reassured to see the mango groves that surrounded the village giving it a pastoral effect and at the same time differentiating it from the dust engulfed villages he had seen *en route*. He was glad to see the spires of the shrines that his grandfather had built. He saw that the women were unveiled. The IAS man accompanying him explained: "Brahmin women" the IAS man whispered, "Very fearless" (254). He met Jussodra, the woman who had come with his grandfather from Trinidad. From her he heard the story of his grandfather's success in Trinidad. He heard how his grandfather had re-established the family, he saw the photographs taken in Trinidad. It ought to have been a final homecoming for Naipaul. But it wasn't. He says, "In a year I had not learned acceptance. I had learned my separateness from India, and was content to be a colonial, without a past, without ancestors" (202). This was once again, a very Indian response. In an attempt to escape the pain of his situation; fearing the loss of unity of his world, Naipaul was ready to flee. He was ready to reject his roots. This is how his visit to his village ends. His meetings with Ramchandra, the head of the family leaves him impatient. He found himself being pressed for money to pay for a litigation to preserve the nineteen acres of his grandfather's land, Naipaul did not offer any financial help. He wished to severe all connections and to flee the village. This is what he eventually does. He leaves the village, refuses to take on a boy who wanted a lift. It was his final attempt at complete retreat: "So it ended, in futility and impatience, a gratuitous act of cruelty, self-reproach and flight" (263). The epilogue titled 'Flight' explains it more fully. Naipaul's distance from India was too great to be bridged. Naipaul fled from India. In London, he tried "in vain, to summon up a positive response to this city where I had lived and worked..." (266). Naipaul's dream of the oblong cloth crystallizes his condition. The oblong cloth was a gift from India. It was an *Indian* gift on account of the affection it so effortlessly contained. But in his dream, the cloth was a mystery. It sought to be "unravelled" (266). Naipaul knew that the clues existed but could not find them. The cloth remained unravelled. This dream in a way sums up Naipaul's predicament of flights and of unravelled labyrinths.

An Area of Darkness has been a classical case of misinterpretation in the West as well as in India. Immediately after its publication, the then Indian government imposed a ban on it. In the West it was hailed as a scathing but truthful vision. The critics on both sides failed to read the book for what it was. It was neither "A masterpiece of travel-writing...wise, original" as Paul Theroux declares on the cover of its Penguin edition nor was it "darkness...people, packed with a kind of life which is death, a negation, distortion and degradation from which he is glad finally to escape."[1] *An Area of Darkness* is to be read as a meeting ground for the homeland and the Diaspora, and therefore, a brief assessment needs to be made of the criticism and applause that the book evoked. In India the criticism was vitriolic. C.D. Narasimhaiah's essay 'Somewhere something has snapped' is a systematic attack on the book. At the beginning of the essay Narasimhaiah declares that Naipaul's assessment of the failings of India cannot be disowned:

> Our failings are so many and so varied that the most patriotic of us cannot defend them. Our love of symbols...rather than of action...our neglect of our great art...unless...approved by European scholars...our endless mimicry....[2]

Narasimhaiah goes on to state that his essay is not intended to be a defence of India, that it is "a sign of maturity in individuals as well as nations to see ourselves as others see us...." He credits Naipaul for a *correct* observation of all that is evident but accuses him of being unable to explore the depth of the Indian mind. As the essay progresses, Narasimhaiah himself makes a very *correct* observation of Naipaul's errors in misinterpretation and misrepresentation but ironically, he is unable to gauge the depth of the darkness or the conflict in the mind of a writer belonging to the Diaspora. H.H. Anniah Gowda sees Naipaul as an "expatriate determined to lambaste India." He finds that "Naipaul, in his reminiscences, has chosen to shut his eyes to the India which is not defecating."[3] Natwar Singh opines:

> It is Mr. Naipaul's unique achievement to have passed that amount of time in India without meeting a single worthwhile human being. He finds fault in almost everything he sees: the people's habits and their manners, the cities, villages, bureaucracy, railways, army. Even the Taj Mahal is not spared.[4]

Naipaul's proposal to transport the Taj Mahal to the United States is interpreted as his hatred of the squalor of India.

What Natwar Singh missed out in his first impassioned response is that Naipaul sought to delink the architectural beauty of the Taj Mahal from its corresponding history, which is painful and cruel. Its beauty can be fully appreciated only when it is cut off from its history. Another extreme is Helen Tiffin's criticism of C.D. Narasimhaiah in which she accuses him of being "intolerant" of any criticism of his country.[5] William Walsh holds that *An Area of Darkness* is "a kind of metaphysical diary of the effort to shine a Western novelist's light into an interior area of darkness."[6]

The main point, which critics on both sides have missed out is the perspective of vision. Visions cannot be divided into airtight compartments of truths and half-truths. Ezekiel's India can never be the India that Naipaul sees.[7] Gail Minault sees Naipaul as a novelist "who has also developed the travel account into a finely honed instrument of personal expression. His attitude sceptical, his vision of human nature sardonic, he cultivates detachment. He is the perpetual, the professional outsider."[8] Sara Suleri found *An Area of Darkness* to be a "fascinating record of delusion."[9]

Naipaul's engagement with India is not a one-way process. It is a complicated case of action and reaction being recorded against a background that is equally complicated. Naipaul has written of his idea of his Hindu-Brahmin self that survived as a small area of "self-deception." He has also recorded that he had been brought up in a double world: the closed Hindu world of his grandmother's family and the outside world. Both these worlds were separate and secret from each other. In India, Naipaul's two selves separated and each self reacted differently to situations at hand. C.D. Narasimhaiah has recorded instances of this fracture in sensibility but has dismissed these as being wilful constructions on the part of the author:

> Attitudes like these have no meaning in the light of the dominant mood of the book. By the time the reader rubs his eyes to take a good look at a flash and say to his neighbour 'behold!,' the jaws of darkness do devour it. It's almost a recurring pattern of the book.[10]

The fact that this alternation in flashes of darkness and light falls into a pattern has more to it than mere posturing. Had Naipaul contrived to block out one side of his response, he would have either ended up as a perfect insider overflowing with warmth or the perfect Catherine Mayo whom he has been so often wrongly compared with. But he did neither. He must be credited for his honesty to his vision, however complicated, however blurred. Naipaul writes of his visit to India to work on *An Area of Darkness*:

> This time I left from England. India was special to England; for two hundred years there had been any number of English travellers' accounts and, latterly, novels. I could not be that kind of traveller. In travelling to India I was travelling to an un-English fantasy, and a fantasy unknown to Indians of India: I was travelling to the peasant India that my Indian grandfathers had sought to re-create in Trinidad, the 'India' I had partly grown up in, the India that was like a loose end in my mind, where our past suddenly stopped. There was no model for me.... To get anywhere in the writing, I had first of all to define myself very clearly to myself. (*EOA* 140-41)

For Naipaul, *An Area of Darkness* was double struggle. It was a struggle to establish a perspective to look at the meaning of India; it was also a struggle to discover the process through which the meaning could be unravelled. The metaphor of an oblong piece of cloth, which was a gift from an Indian friend, explains his inability to find an end to his double struggle. The book ends in ambivalence. There could have been no other possible ending. The book is dappled all over but the areas of darkness and light cannot be interpreted as belonging to a Western or an Eastern sensibility. The area of darkness, as Naipaul has defined at the onset, is that aspect of India or that aspect of Indian sensibility which remains impenetrable for him. The area of light is the area of his "experience, in time and place" (*AD* 30). It is clearly a division of experience into broad categories of what is comprehensible and what is not. Naipaul, in his own words has accepted that he has been unable to express his briefly grasped understanding of the philosophy that is at the heart of India: "I felt it as something true which I could never adequately express and never seize again" (266-67).

The point that calls for an explanation is the difference in Naipaul's India and the India of his Indian critics. Numerous writers had written about India before Naipaul did, and not always sympathetically. A Beverly Nicholas or a Catherine Mayo could be dismissed for being *incapable* of understanding India. Their vision could be ignored because they were, after all, *foreigners.* What did they know of India? But with Naipaul, Indians felt betrayed. *He* was expected to know and to understand. The division of experience had occurred three generations ago. Naipaul was an outsider in India. His critics were outsiders to his experience. Naipaul's perception and portrayal of India, if seen in this light, is a unique record of the division of sensibility that has become a permanent paradigm of our times.

The value of *An Area of Darkness* is that the book and its critique have documented the confusion and alienation that are the legacies of the Empire. Never before was India presented through a diasporic vision. Never before had the Indians in India been exposed to the pain and agony of such a vision, so much so, that within India even the veracity of Naipaul's experience was very often questioned. *An Area of Darkness* stands today as the first stage of a diasporic writer's problematic relation with the country of his origin: it abounds in confusions and contradictions; there is no potent thesis about India. There are recurrent notes of the writer's identification with India at a personal level. He did not want India "to sink." And so, the writer returns with more books on India attempting an analysis of its problems and pens the growth of his experience.

3

CONFRONTING HISTORY

> India in the late twentieth century still seems so much itself, so rooted in its own civilization, it takes time to understand that its independence has meant more than the going away of the British; that the India to which Independence came was a land of far older defeat.
>
> V.S. Naipaul, *India: A Wounded Civilization.*

V.S. Naipaul's second book on India, *India: A Wounded Civilization,* marks the second stage in the development of his diasporic concerns. This book attempts to find an answer to the questions that raged all over *An Area of Darkness.* It tries to gauge what is the "something" that has snapped, and where, and how, and why (*AD* 207). As compared to *An Area of Darkness,* this book is more analytical in tone. The chaotic alteration between acceptance and rejection of India in the earlier book is replaced by an ordered and organized search through history, sociology, politics and literature. However, it is similar to *An Area of Darkness* in its point of beginning. This book too begins with the author and his mental make-up. That is how the perspective is defined as a diasporic one:

> India is for me a difficult country. It isn't my home and cannot be my home; and yet I cannot reject it or be indifferent to it; I cannot travel only for the sights. I am at once too close and too far.... A hundred years had been enough to wash me clear of many Indian religious attitudes; and without these attitudes the distress of India was—and is—almost insupportable. It has taken me much time...to define what separates me from the country; and to

> understand how far the 'Indian' attitudes of someone like myself...have diverged from the attitudes of people to whom India is still whole. (*WC* 9)

From the 'Foreword' two things are very clear. First, the perspective is a diasporic one and the book ought to be examined in that light. Second, the method of enquiry would also centre round the author and *his* understanding of the history, society and literature of India, which would be *different* from the way rooted Indians look at these. The book is divided into eight chapters that are classified under three major parts which in turn mark the three major movements in the writer's development of a prognosis about the maladies that ail India.

The first part titled 'An Old Equilibrium' is an analysis of the psychology behind the eternal "continuity" of India. Taking the example of the ancient kingdom of Vijaynagar, Naipaul unravels the systematic destruction of the kingdom that led to a permanent loss of human talent and intellectual capacity. This in turn also led to a loss of historical sense. In this way the destruction was rendered complete and irreversible. A flourishing civilization contracted with each conquest and in the end, having no more reality to survive on, it drew on legend for sustenance. All the memories of terrible violence were forgotten and the only memories that survived were fabulous renderings of the glory of the past, before the coming of the conquerors. The remnants of the monuments survived: irrigation canals, palaces, a temple with rows of musical stone columns that could be played, a broken aqueduct, the ruins of a bridge. But the talent that had designed and built these had been wiped out. The kingdom of Vijaynagar stood as an area officially declared "backward," with plans for its development underway. Life continued, pilgrims still thronged the ancient temple and in that, the continuity of India seemed to maintain itself. But this continuity was just a facade, a covering for the terrible rupture that had occurred with the loss of history, of creative expertise and of human energy.

Naipaul sees this contradiction repeating itself throughout the country. Each time India was attacked, it lost its intellectual life and survived on legends of the past. A repeated process like this made India "archaic" because knowledge and talent was continually lost (18). As in Vijaynagar, in the rest of India too, this resulted in a big gap between the talent behind its ancient monuments and cities and the deficiencies of the people who now inhabited these once flourishing areas. For ages, this gap lay covered by the outward "continuity." But with the coming of Independence, with the coming of five-year plans, with the programmes for development of "backward" areas, this facade was blown off and the cracks and fissures showed. Indian nationalism had evoked the Indian past but post-independence development schemes were forward looking. National pride was directly linked to the glorious past. The glory of the present was yet to be built. This contradiction "cracked the civilization open" (18). The institutions for growth and development were borrowed ones and were therefore not bringing about desired results. The past, once so revered, was unable to provide an alternative for borrowed institutions and this was the crisis of India. Referring to the Emergency Naipaul says:

> The turbulence in India this time hasn't come from foreign invasion or conquest; it has been generated from within.... The crisis of India is not only political or economic. The larger crisis is of a wounded old civilization that has at last become aware of its inadequacies and is without the intellectual means to move ahead. (18)

Naipaul sees the crisis of India as the beginning of the loss of an old equilibrium. Earlier in the chapter he had identified this equilibrium as being a mere facade to cover up a great imbalance. Although Naipaul *does not say it*, the disruption of this equilibrium and the consequent crisis can only be the beginning of a positive development. Naipaul has built up on this in his next book on India, which will be discussed in Chapter 4. Another example of the old equilibrium is drawn from literature. Naipaul sees R.K. Narayan's unexamined sense of continuity as being a typically Hindu "simplification of reality" (21).

He had earlier read Narayan's novels as social comedies. He now sees Narayan's works to be more akin to Hindu religious fables. A detailed analysis of *Mr. Sampath* follows.

Here Naipaul sees in the character of its hero, Srinivas a misinterpretation of the ideas of *karma* and non-violence. Srinivas, a reader of the *Upanishads* has read the same meaning into the Hindu idea of *nishkaam karma* as the equivalent of "non doing." The Hindu idea advocates that a person must perform his *karma* without thinking or yearning for benefits, which are only illusions. It does not mean that a person should withdraw from all action. The dividing line is very thin and elastic. And so Srinivas slips conveniently into non-action. The Gandhian idea of nonviolence was not passivity it was a form of action. This too is misread by Srinivas as "non doing, non-interference, social indifference" (25). He resorts to a "form of self-cherishing" which is totally dependent on the action of others. "It depends on the continuing activity of others...the rupees arriving from somewhere" (23). Naipaul finds such an idea of religious surrender as being parasitic and degenerate. In the fate of Srinivas, Naipaul sees the fate of the vast Indian populace that had interpreted its religious philosophy in such a way that the equilibrium of their idea of themselves was maintained. They accepted distress as the divinely ordained predicament of humankind.

In the same vein Naipaul records his impressions of the farm workers and labourers of North Bihar and Rajasthan. Bihar, which was once "the cultural heartland" of India remained filled with cruelty and poverty more than two decades after Independence. The people did not question. They had a resigned acceptance of suffering and poverty. Such total resignation left little ground for thoughts of change. In Rajasthan Naipaul saw two different examples of how 'development' had come to the state. He saw dams and irrigation schemes being worked on to remove their technical faults. In a model village he saw peasantry involved in acquiring latest agricultural expertise. There was electricity in the village and all other outward signs of development. But the women were excluded from all this. They withdrew under their veils when the commissioner started one of his important discussions. In Bundi, which was once a centre of art and had its own school of painting, Naipaul found that all its vitality had vanished. The Bundi castle was in a state of decay; the people of Bundi saw themselves as being completely dependent on the power of the authority and did nothing more than putting up an elaborate show of their deference to authority. They were "less amenable to the commissioner's ideas" (31). They were secure in their condition and the only passion that could move them was a passion for honour. Apart from this, they could not be moved to any form of action. Their world was lost and in order to maintain that old equilibrium, they had "retreated to their last, impregnable defences: their knowledge of who they were, their caste, their *karma*, their unshakable place in the scheme of things" (32).

This was universally true for all Indians. For the Prince, who had lost his privy purse, for the woman who had married a foreigner, and for the vast majority that lived in villages and in towns. To them, India was a truth. Whatever happened to them happened in compliance to some divine master plan beyond human comprehension. India was not to be judged. It was beyond that. In this idea lay the foundations of the age-old equilibrium, which Indians conceived as the proof of the eternal continuity of India. Naipaul attacks this idea in the next chapter, 'The Shattering World.' He begins by quoting R.K. Narayan—"India will go on"; and finds that even in the face of a crisis like the Emergency, the illusion of the old equilibrium survived. But there had been a change. Naipaul identifies this change in R.K. Narayan's journey from *Mr. Sampath* to *The Vendor of Sweets*. The sweet-vendor Jagan is a Gandhian, a pious Hindu, who has worked for the Independence of India. But he does not pay his sales tax. In the first place, Jagan has no idea of what Independence or self-governance means. He cheats the very same government for whose sake he had bravely taken police beatings during the British rule. His idea of the nation is limited to his idea of Gandhi. Narayan jokes that if *Gandhi* had asked people to pay their sales tax, Jagan would have surely done so. Naipaul sees in this double consciousness of Jagan a decadent idea of Hindu morality: "how many Jagans exist who, conscious only of their Gandhian piety, their personal virtue, have mocked and undermined the Independence for which they say they have worked!" (39). Naipaul's thesis is that the old equilibrium has shattered with the world opening up (entry of Jagan's son with his foreign girlfriend). Independent India calls for a different kind of devotion in order to bring about progress. The old pastoral world cannot be re-established. Jagan's world and ideologies could only spell more Emergencies for India. India needed to invest in science and industry. The "satire on 'modern' civilization" in *The Vendor of Sweets* is a proof of the violation the shattering of the unity of the world in the fragile lives of people like Jagan (42). Jagan's only purpose in his life was to maintain his own idea of purity, his own idea of Gandhianism. His fairness to his customers arose out of his idea of himself being pure and true and not because of any concern to the society, to the people. His idea of his world was restricted and fragile and so it broke. Jagan fled the world in anguish. His renunciation was not the calm, composed and self-willed renunciation advocated by Hindu philosophy. He found himself at a point of no return. He fled. This was the final shattering of the old world.

The Emergency was also a symptom of the problem of the dismantling of the old world. It was a proof that the society had broken down. Unfortunately, in India it was seen as a mere political crisis "which it was in the power of Mrs. Gandhi or the opposition to resolve" (45). The newspapers, already censored, mainly concerned themselves with news of raids and arrests of people charged with economic offences. However, the Emergency did not attempt to set things right. It showed off terror but "established no new moral frame...it held out no promise for a better regulated future. It reinforced, if anything...the need to hide and hoard" (45). The problem needed a deeper resolution. Naipaul traces the chaos of the Emergency to the blunders that had followed Independence. The Jagans whose commitment to a kind of a "holy war" under Gandhi had won India its independence, were rendered directionless after independence. They had no idea of responsibility to the state and in the absence of any other means to include them in the process of growth, they had returned to their old world which was self-centred. Like Jagan, they thought that the government would function in some magical way with no contribution or involvement from them. They had no idea of what democracy required of them as citizens. The very idea was alien; they thought that as always, "India would go on" (37). But when it didn't, they didn't know what to do. However, the shattering of the old equilibrium was not to be seen as negative. It was a positive beginning:

> With Independence and growth, chaos and a loss of faith, India was awakening to its distress and the cruelties that had always lain below its apparent stability, its capacity simply for going on.... The old equilibrium had gone.... But out of this chaos, out of the crumbling of the old Hindu system, and the spirit of rejection, India was learning new ways of seeing and feeling. (48)

The last section of the chapter reflects on the spirit of rejection. Naipaul finds the plays of Vijay Tendulkar dealing with this theme. *The Vultures* is about the end of all reverences. With the new opportunity of making money, the old values are lost and people become more individualistic. There is "no pure past, and religion can provide no retreat" (49). Tendulkar's plays mark a change in the Indian sensibility. The hero of *Sakharam Binder* is a low caste man who works as a binder for a living. He has rejected all those things which an Indian society holds dear. He has rejected caste, religion, clan and family. He has not married but lives with "other men's discarded wives, whom he rescues from temples or streets" (50). His only faith lies in honesty. At the end of the play he is destroyed but Tendulkar has portrayed him as a hero. Sakharam Binder's rebellion is thus a big leap from the rebellion of Jagan's son in *The Vendor of Sweets.* Naipaul describes his meeting with Tendulkar and in it he finds another example of the fact that, for India, there could be no more retreats. Tendulkar, while working on a book on violence in India had travelled to various parts of the country. In Bihar he had seen things, which "he had never believed existed" (50). But in his conversation, he talked of the beauty of the Ganga and did not refer to the tragic sights on its banks, in the villages and towns through which it flowed. Even Tendulkar with his new sensibility wanted to escape the horrors. He too yearned for retreat into the calmness of the old order in which these horrors didn't show up. This past couldn't be claimed now. The past in itself hadn't been an egalitarian one. It "enslaved one quarter of the population" as low caste or untouchables (53). By doing this, it fragmented the society. These fragmented parts were as directionless as the rest of the people and India was in chaos. This is how the first section of the book defines India—as a land repeatedly wounded, now facing a revolt from the very same forces that once held it together.

The next section, 'A New Claim on Land' records an undercurrent of movement in the middle and lower middle classes of India. The two chapters that make up this section deal with the movement of the village population towards the metropolises and the creation of the new working class. 'The Skyscrapers and the Chawls' draws a contrast between the advancement of industrialized Bombay and the contradiction of un-accommodated workforce that makes its industries run. On one hand are the industries that need labour. On the other is the problem of accommodation. The workforce that comes from nearby villages spills on the streets and pavements at night. "The poor are needed as hands, as labour. But the city was not built to accommodate them" (58). Glamorous skyscrapers provide a majestic sight at night. In their shadows live the chawl and pavement dwellers. Chawls were originally meant to accommodate the workers in the numerous textile mills of Bombay. Whatever be the constricting effects of chawl life, to own a chawl was to be established. There were other, poorer classes of workers who did not even have access to the constricted chawl life. These people made their own colonies—squatters' settlements. Over the years, their settlements had grown into more organized residential areas and they had attached themselves to the Shiv Sena—the army named after the Maratha leader Shivaji. Naipaul notices a kind of movement here. At the very grass-root level there was an attempt at a more organized community living. The interests of the individual in particular and the community in general were taken care of.

The settlements had Shiv Sena's committee offices which were "dedicated as much to municipal self-regulation as to the Sena's politics: industrial workers beginning to apply something of the discipline of the factory floor to the areas where they lived" (64). Sena politics worked at different levels.

Apart from political power, it inspired in the people at the bottom of the social ladder a sense of self-respect and belonging. The Sena committees, which were mostly run by enthusiastic young men, worked at improving the quality of life of the chawl and settlement dwellers and thereby also consolidated political goodwill and loyalty. Amidst all this movement towards a better life, Naipaul has noticed that the static rigidity of the relation between caste and work had remained as such. Although the settlements were provided with municipal washing areas and community lavatories, the task of cleaning up was left to the municipal sweeper. When the sweeper didn't turn up, people just closed their eyes to the filth and continued with their life.

The Shiv Sena had its own political complications. "The Sena 'army' is xenophobic," says Naipaul (62). On its agenda was a Maharashtra only for those born of Maharashtrian parents. On account of its great popularity with the masses, the Sena wielded tremendous political power. Its leader had revived the cult of Shivaji and had thus evoked in the masses, feelings of self-respect and power:

> ...the Sena is a great contracting out, not from India but from a Hindu system, which, in the conditions of today, in the conditions of industrial Bombay, has at last been felt to be inadequate. It is in part a reworking of the Hindu system. Men do not accept chaos; they ceaselessly seek to remake their world; they reach out for such ideas as are accessible and fit their need. (63)

The Sena had built for itself a very large base because it aligned itself with the cause of the vast masses of the urban poor, which doubled and redoubled continuously. Naipaul observed that although the major movement in Bombay seemed to be urbanization—the coming up of skyscrapers and industries, the actual movement was taking place at a lower level. The dimensions of this grass-root movement were tremendous because it had begun to give the people an idea of themselves:

> For the Sena man, and the people they led, the world was new; they saw themselves at the beginning of things:

> unaccommodated men making a claim on their land for the first time, and out of chaos evolving their own philosophy of community and self-help. (72)

This chapter marks a sharp shift in Naipaul's earlier observations of Bombay that he had made in *An Area of Darkness*. In the character of the engineer who had taken him to the squatters' settlements, he saw a genuine vision, foresight and dedication. The next chapter 'The House of Grain' also depicts a positive movement. This movement was evident in the new development of Poona and also in the co-operative irrigation scheme being laid down in a nearly village. Movement was to be seen in the 'graduate' daughter-in-law in the Patel's house, in people waiting for the morning bus, in the zeal of the enterprising but shortsighted restaurateur turned water supplier who accepted chapatis in lieu of cash. There was movement here—in the co-operative digging of the lift-canal and in the restaurateur's water supply but this movement was less than productive. The efforts of the very thin man digging his part of the trench or of the veiled Rajasthani woman brushing the dust with a rag could have easily been rendered more effective and more productive by the application of simple mechanical skills.

Naipaul's visit to a village and his meeting with the village sarpanch and the Patel laid bare a major reason in the unequal development of India. In this part of the chapter, Naipaul takes a close look at the social mechanism of the rural Indian society. The Patel, the biggest landowner in the village continued to be the traditional symbol of power. The elected sarpanch, who ought to have been the head of the village, was a mere puppet. The traditional loyalty to the Patel continued. He was the actual master. Independence had not changed much. His house had all amenities "Electric light, ready water, an outhouse: the Patel was the only man in the village to possess them all..." (86). He owned land and he nearly owned the labourers that he employed to work on his land. Villagers were resigned to the fact that "what was for the Patel couldn't be for them" (85). That the Patel was progressive and not opposed to cooperative projects such as the irrigation scheme was a bonus, a mark of his charitable and benign nature for which the villagers were thankful:

> It was necessary to be in the village, to see the Patel and his attendants, to understand the nature of power of that simple man, to see how easily such a man could, if he wished, frustrate the talk from Delhi about minimum wages, the abolition of untouchability, the abolition of rural indebtedness. How could the laws be enforced? Who would be the policeman in this village? (86)

Independence had brought development but that development had touched people unequally. The old pattern of the landed masters and landless labourers continued. Democracy and Panchayati Raj became toys in the hands of traditional power wielders. Officials, politicians and administrators were sucked into the pattern of the ruler and the ruled. Worse still, the instruments of democracy could easily be turned into instruments of a more organized oppression. Naipaul has explained the incessant flow of people towards the cities in this context. The people coming to cities were "fleeing not only from landlessness but also from tyranny, the rule in a thousand villages of men like the Patel and the sarpanch" (89).

Another form of escape from oppression was to be found in the origin of communities of dacoits in central and North-western India. Naipaul does not explain this phenomenon in detail but moves on to yet another attempt at an escape from oppression—the Naxalbari movement in Bengal and Andhra. He calls it a "tragic attempt at a revolution" (89). The tragedy of the Naxalbari movement was that it could not explain its ideology to a people so used to "reverencing a Master and used for centuries to the idea of *karma*" (92). The ideology inevitably degenerated into the "idea of the enemy" and was lost:

> Naxalism was an intellectual tragedy, a tragedy of idealism, ignorance and mimicry: middle-class India, after the Gandhian upheaval, incapable of generating ideas and institutions of its own, needing constantly in the modern world to be inducted into the art, science, and ideas of other civilizations, not always understanding the consequences, and this time borrowing something deadly, somebody else's idea of revolution. (93)

'A New Claim on the Land' sees India on the move. The movement came into being because the cities and the industries gave people an alternative to escape the predicament of a humiliating and oppressed existence as landless poor in the Patel-centric agrarian set up. Naipaul holds that any study of India that does not take into account this movement at the grass-roots is "worthless." This movement marked a great shift from the ideas that ruled the country immediately after independence:

> The poor are no longer the occasion for sentiment or holy almsgiving; land reform no longer a matter for the religious conscience. (93)

The four chapters in the last section titled 'Not Ideas, but Obsessions' deal with conflicting ideas. The common thread that holds these four chapters together is the idea of India as a people struggling amidst their ambivalences, as victims of mimicry, as people incapacitated by borrowed institutions for so long that any original action could not be possible. Naipaul begins with Gandhi. He furthers the analysis of Gandhi that he had made in *An Area of Darkness.* Naipaul presents an original interpretation of the victories and failures of Gandhi. He attempts to find out the reason behind Gandhi's great success in pre-independence times, his shattering failure immediately afterwards and subsequent degeneration of his ideas and ideals. Naipaul's quarrel with Gandhi is that he energized a people in an unprecedented manner and created a form of struggle to which the Indian psyche could easily relate. But having done that, he had left the energized nation to itself. He had shaken up a sleeping civilization but had not taught it to observe, analyse and understand itself. He had built a nation of followers with no leadership. All that remained in the name of leadership was endless mimicry.

Gandhi's inward looking philosophy sustained him, but it could not sustain India. What would happen to a nation of inward looking people to whom the outer world mattered only up to that extent to which it affected the inner? This, says Naipaul, was Gandhi's defect of vision. Naipaul traces the seeds of this short-sightedness in Gandhi's selective "blindness" to those external incidents or landscapes, which were not directly connected to his inner sphere of experience, understanding or development:

> Gandhi's self-absorption was part of his strength. Without it he would have done nothing and might even have been destroyed. But with this self-absorption there was, as always, a kind of blindness. (100)

Quoting Sudhir Kakar, Naipaul concludes that the relationship of Indians to their outside world is more akin to a childhood stage when the person relates to the world through the mother. Similarly, Indians always turn inwards, seeking the security of a life ordered by society. Left on his own, the individual is lost because he has no idea of himself. He can project himself only through the security of an ordered society with its lists of rules and rituals. Gandhi harnessed this unquestioning faith in truth and religion and baffled the British, but he did not know how to carry on. Independence was won, the enemy was defeated and the nation sat itself down in anticipation of a *Ramrajya*—a rule by Ram. To a people so used to being governed, the idea of *swaraj*, self-governance did not strike home. So post-independence India withdrew into itself waiting for things to take care of themselves, waiting for *Ramrajya* to descend on the country. Taking the example of the character of the Acharya from U.R. Anantamurti's novel *Samskara*, Naipaul explains the great Indian reliance on non-action. The Acharya, a learned man, had not learnt to analyse situations and offer solutions. He was content to scan books for answers; he had a greater belief in God's decision that would, through the mystical falling of the flower, make itself known to him. Meeting failure in both cases, the Acharya is lost. People like the Acharya lead "instinctive lives, crippled by rules...they make up a society without a head" (109).

Had Naipaul been content to dismiss Gandhi and critique the Acharya, he could have been written off as a casual observer who had no knowledge or understanding of India or of Gandhi. But Naipaul attempts a study and an analysis of what differentiated Gandhi from the teeming millions that he led.

> But there is an important difference. The Acharya is imprisoned in his dead civilization; he can only define himself within it. He has not, like Gandhi in England, had to work out his faith and decide where—in the wider world—he stands. (110)

Unlike the Acharya, Gandhi believed in action. Amidst the chaotic turbulence of energies released by him, that he is no longer able to control, Gandhi in Noakhali realizes that he has "nothing to offer except his presence" (111). He realizes that his philosophy was not equipped to deal with this new turn of events. But unlike the Acharya, Gandhi did not seek escape in non-action, in passivity:

> ...Noakhali. Sad last pilgrimage: embittered people scatter broken glass on the roads he is to walk...he has nothing to offer except his presence, and he knows it. Yet he is heard to say to himself again and again, '*Kya Karun*? *Kya Karun*? What shall I do?' At this terrible moment his thoughts are of action, and he is magnificent. (111)

Naipaul holds that Gandhi, on account of his sensitivity to external experience, saw India very objectively. He knew how the Indian qualities of complacency, tolerance and faith in religion could be positively used. It spelt immediate success. But Gandhi could not foresee the shortcomings of his method. He had taken people out of their traditional decadent world of caste, class, clan and religion, and had shown them a goal: independence. People followed in his wake and substituted their old-world unity with 'Gandhianism.' Newer ones like the spinning-wheel, replaced their old rituals. The pattern continued, the symbols changed. Gandhi's defect of vision was that he took the people out of their world but did not teach them to look at themselves as individuals:

> When men cannot observe, they don't have ideas: they have obsessions. When people live instinctive lives, something like a collective amnesia steadily blurs the past. (112)

One man's short-sightedness led a nation astray because it was this one man's vision that had set it in motion.

Emergency was the logical fallout of rampant confusion, of "Individual obsessions" turning into "political movements" (114). The next chapter 'Synthesis and Mimicry' interrogates the classic Indian claim that India, over the years, has always successfully assimilated diverse influences. Naipaul's first attack is on 'intermediate technology,' which was supposed to provide a link between the advanced scientific methods and the conventional agrarian methods employed in India. This 'intermediate technology' had turned itself into futile experiments edging on absurdity—the wired up bull, the harvesting shoes, foot operated harvesting shears and so on. It was a needless complication of otherwise simple agricultural tools and served no productive purpose. It was not synthesis but an intellectual confusion and that too in an institution that was meant to contribute to national development. The only direct evidence of cultural synthesis was to be found in the pre-British schools of painting.

With the coming of the British, the break with the past was final. Old wisdom, old knowledge, traditional craftsmanship and architecture died out. There was no synthesis, no assimilation but a complete incongruous replacement. The proof is there in the climatically ill-suited tourist guesthouse of Jaisalmer, in the thoughtlessly designed roof of the modern airport building in Ahmedabad. The East-West encounter that occurred after the coming of the British was superficial because there was no Indian tradition to receive the new influences. The Indian tradition, the basic medium to accept new influences, did not exist and the influences themselves stuck out absurdly. Synthesis was reduced to mimicry:

> The Indian past can no longer provide inspiration for the Indian present...the West is too dominant, and too varied; and India continues imitative and insecure.... India, without its own living traditions, has lost the ability to incorporate and adapt; what it borrows it seeks to swallow whole. For all its appearance of cultural continuity, for all the liveliness of its arts of dance, music, and cinema, India is incomplete: a whole creative side has died. It is the price India has had to pay for its British period. (126)

Naipaul sees India functioning on borrowed institutions. The press, the education system, the judiciary are all borrowed and stand as obstacles in the people's perception of themselves and their idea of India. The Indian press did not seek to put India "in touch with itself," the Indian judicial system designed by the British could not perform "the law's constant reassessing, reforming role" (132). The law steers clear of the numerous misinterpretations of *dharma* that are in circulation:

> The law avoids the collision with *dharma*. Yet it is this *dharma* that the law must grapple with if the law is to have a 'dynamic role.' (134)

India needs to step out of its comfort zone of explaining its incongruities and contradictions as "synthesis." It has to abandon its imported ideas and ideologies, it has to question and arrive at an understanding of itself. And for that, India needs to shed its policy of total acceptance and complacency. 'Paradise Lost' records people's reaction to the emergency imposed by Indira Gandhi. It also records the confused agenda of the opposition and its even more confused line of action. Political sterility was complete. There was neither *swaraj* nor *Ramrajya*. Gandhianism was reduced to a show of khadi and long impassioned speeches and the people, simply waited for things to take care of themselves.

The last chapter is a question mark. Titled 'Renaissance or Continuity,' it once again examines the reasons behind the failure of Gandhianism and its caricatured version being upheld through a series of acts of mimicry. In Vinoba Bhave, Naipaul sees a "mimic mahatma" whose actions had not served India in any way. The living evidence of the futility of such mimicry is Bihar where Bhave had performed much of his land-gift walk schemes:

> Once, on the march, he said that untouchables did work human beings shouldn't do; for that reason they should be given land, to become tillers.... The whole point of Gandhi's message was lost. (166)

Bhave's life was thus a parody of Gandhi without actual involvement or vision for the causes at hand. Bhave believed that walks and fasts would solve all problems. He did not know the practical reason behind Gandhi's walks and marches. Gandhi's marches connected people to ideas at a time when communication and commutation were both difficult. Bhave's marches overlooked that. The concept of *dharma* degenerated. Through years of conquest and oppression, it came to be associated with unquestioning servitude and patient suffering. The only way to claim past glory was to be found in intellectual development. India must shed its longing for a past that it hardly understands. The past is just a glorious abstraction because with the amnesias that followed each conquest, India lost touch with itself:

> While India tries to go back to an idea of its past, it will not possess that past or be enriched by it. The past can now be possessed only by inquiry and scholarship, by intellectual rather than spiritual discipline. The past has to be seen to be dead; or the past will kill. (174)

Naipaul has, in this book attempted an analysis of the problems and complications of India and has in the process, once again stirred up a hornet's nest. The reactions are typical and follow the same pattern as those that were evoked by *An Area of Darkness.* As stated at the beginning of the chapter, the perspective of the writer as diasporic is emphasized and the method of enquiry centres round *his* perception which is obviously very different from the rooted Indian perspective.

Helga Chaudhary suggested that Naipaul name his book *Hindu India: A Wounded Civilization.*[1] The fact of the forced mass conversions during the Mughal period and the consequent rupture in the social fabric has been conveniently overlooked in the above statement. Indians, as of now, whether Hindus, Muslims or Christians share a common pain of rupture. Naipaul has concentrated on that point of rupture rather than on the difference in sensibilities of Hindu Indians and Muslim Indians. Fawzia Mustafa holds that "Naipaul's habits of evaluation still rely upon the historically unreliable synecdochal narrative techniques of reporting random interviews... clippings from newspaper accounts...local novels...political biographies."[2] The validity of Naipaul's evidence can be questioned on the basis of truth of historical fact. But the question here is not of the truth or validity of a fact or an ideology. Naipaul is recording contemporary India and is therefore using as his base material contemporary versions of fact. The speeches of politicians, the articles in newspapers are all contemporary versions of facts and can lay bare the gap between the original idea and the currency that it has come to acquire. For example, Naipaul quotes from the *Times of India*, a speech by the then Prime Minister, Mrs. Indira Gandhi in which she equates law with dharma and urges people to uphold dharma (*WC* 132). Naipaul here uses the current connotation of he term *dharma* and not its vedantic original meaning.

Naipaul's reliance on what Mustafa terms as "historically unreliable" sources serves his purpose of marking out areas where original knowledge has been disfigured and is in a state of decay. Dilip Chitre's criticism of Naipaul, on the surface, seems to be more dispassionate than that of most Indian critics.[3] However, the forces that are at work within Naipaul in his account of India are also at work in Chitre's account of Naipaul. His objection is that the likes of Naipaul treat India as an aesthetic object. On one hand Chitre finds that Naipaul's "enterprise is not wholly in the wrong direction; only his methods are questionable and his information too thin" (186). On the other hand he questions the very validity of Naipaul's "enterprise" by commenting that Naipaul's failure lies in his decision to attempt an accurate and factual portrayal of a civilization. "Naipaul's failure, I think, stems from a fallacy most creative writers are prone to commit. They treat nations, civilizations...not as the fictional bodies and myths that they are but as if they had a being of their own..." (186). Dilip Chitre's argument spares Dr. Sudhir Kakar's theory of the "underdeveloped ego" because it would not be fair to Dr. Kakar if his hypotheses were discussed on the basis of Naipaul's accounts. Chitre easily evades the issue and falls into the stereotypical Indian response to Naipaul: "THE OBVIOUS BANALITIES of Indian public life do not need an exalted visiting mind like Naipaul's for a detailed savaging" (186). Other critics were suspicious of his intentions and damned him as a "despicable lackey of neo-colonialism."[4] Sudha Rai provides one of the most consistent and detailed studies of Naipaul's engagement with India. She has analysed in great detail Naipaul's understanding of Gandhi and Gandhianism as the interaction of "a Hindu self and a Western self in Naipaul."[5] However, even Rai begins her analysis of Naipaul's perception of Gandhi thus: "What astounds us is Naipaul's near-total lack of self-consciousness in the comments on Gandhi..." (50). This mild annoyance with a lack of proper self-consciousness, of proper awe on Naipaul's part, coming from a critic, is equally astounding. Self-consciousness, of all things is certainly the least desirable element in an analysis. Rai's statement in a way vindicates Naipaul's stand that Gandhi in India is meant to be reverenced, he is never to be questioned, never to be analysed and consequently, never to be understood. Naipaul has been wrongly implicated for advocating a break from the past. This is a misreading of his statement that "The past *has to be seen* to be dead; or the past will kill" (*WC* 174, italics mine). It is not an advocacy of a clean break from the past. It is an advocacy of the acceptance of the fact that the inadequacy and blunders of the past have to be recognized and the present has to be safeguarded against those. The past *has to be seen.* A blind reversal to glorious abstractions of the past can in no way help India establish itself in the present. "Intellectual discipline" can revive old knowledge, old art, in a way "spiritual discipline" cannot. In 1986 Naipaul wrote, "Men need history; it helps them to have an idea of who they are" (*EOA* 318). But history has to be *seen* and not to be blindly accepted and eulogised to abstraction. The past has to be continuously monitored, it has to be regularly weeded and the weeds of the past—the errors, the degenerations, need to be extracted and displayed for public scorn. The past, if allowed to grow un-weeded would choke the present.

Like *An Area of Darkness, India: A Wounded Civilization* was also largely misunderstood in the West. Naipaul was hailed for having a very clear perception of the problems of India. The blurb on the book says it all. For Gordon Rohler,

Naipaul's irony enabled him "to examine his past without any sentimental self-indulgence."[6] William Walsh found Naipaul's irony to be "the agent of mediation between experience and vision" and he placed Naipaul in the great tradition of the English novel.[7] The misunderstanding is not only colossal but also typical of the First World's condescending attitudes. *India: A Wounded Civilization* marks the second stage in the diasporic writer's engagement with the land of his origin. The vision is diasporic because Naipaul brings to India those very ideas of India that he was already familiar with: R.K. Narayan, Gandhi, *dharma* and *karma*. Once in India, he builds upon these ideas. This is the reason why *India: A Wounded Civilization* can neither be like Sunil Khilnani's *The Idea of India* nor like Sashi Tharoor's *India: From Midnight to the Millennium*. Naipaul's main concern is with people's idea of themselves, with rural indebtedness, with caste and class obsessions. He sees history as dead and sterile, incapable of generating any kind of revival. These attributes are directly linked to Naipaul's experience of the Indian society in Trinidad. The people there had blocked out all connections with their indentured past. Rural indebtedness and landlessness had landed them up in Trinidad. The caste and class obsessions survived all amnesias. They lost their sense of history but did not lose their sense of caste. It was their ultimate defence. Thus Naipaul's concerns in *India: A Wounded Civilization* are primarily based on his personal and inherited experiences as a member of the Diaspora. Sudha Rai wrote in 1982 that India will beckon to Naipaul, again and again, until "the whole trick was undone" (*AD* 266). That is exactly what has happened. In *India: A Wounded Civilization* Naipaul observed a number of ideas, ideologies, plans and schemes but the only observation that struck home and remained with him was his idea of "The millions...on the move" (*WC* 93). Amidst his despair for the nullity of the current brand of Gandhianism and *dharma* he saw regenerative hope in the positive movement of the common people. In this way, the foundation for *India: A Million Mutinies Now* was laid.

Naipaul's concerns with the identity crisis and degeneration caused by the stalling of Hindu India under Mughal conquests are not limited to *India: A Wounded Civilization*. He is intellectually committed to his cause, which is to analyse various aspects of the maladies that have reduced India's once glorious past to its dismal present. Naipaul's response to the demolition of the Babri Masjid is in tune with Naipaul's thesis in *India: A Wounded Civilization*. Naipaul holds that Hindu India invited conquests and finds that this drawing upon the Hindu past in the present times has led to the creation of a new sense of identity:

> Individual obsessions coalesce into political movements; and in the last ten years or so these movements of protest have become wilder. Many of these movements look back to the past, which they reinterpret to suit their needs. Some, like the Shiv Sena in Bombay (looking back two and a half centuries to the period of Maratha glory) and the Dravidian movement in the south (seeking to revenge itself, after three thousand years, on the Aryan north), have positive regenerating effects. (*WC* 114)

After the demolition of the Babri Masjid, Naipaul declared that his observations in *India: A Wounded Civilization* remained valid. He saw the demolition as a very small part of the vast change in the Hindus' idea of themselves and as an attempt to retrieve their identity of the pre-Islamic period. He saw in it the seed for a greater "intellectual transformation" of India provided it was kept safe from the hands of the fanatics:

> The people who say that there was no temple there are missing the point. Babar, you must understand, had contempt for the country he had conquered. And his building that mosque was an act of contempt. In Ayodhya the construction of a mosque on a spot regarded as sacred by the conquered population was meant as an insult to an ancient idea, the idea of Ram which was two or three thousand years old. One needs to understand the passion that took (the kar-sevaks) on top of the domes. The jeans and tee-shirts are superficial. The passion alone is real. You can't dismiss it. You have to try and harness it. Hitherto in India the thinking has come from the top. What is happening now is different. The movement is from below.

> What is happening in India is a new, historical awakening. It seems to me that Indians are becoming alive to their history. Romila Thapar's book on Indian History is a Marxist attitude which in substance says: there is a higher truth behind the invasions, feudalism and all that. The correct truth is the way the invaders looked at their (own) actions. They were conquering, they were subjugating. And they were in a country where people never understood this. Only now are the people beginning to understand that there has been a great vandalising of India. Because of the nature of the conquest and the nature of Hindu society such understanding had eluded Indians before. What is happening in India is a highly creative process. Indian intellectuals, who want to be secure in their liberal beliefs, may not understand what is going on,.... But every other Indian knows precisely what is happening: deep down he knows that a larger response is emerging even if at times this response appears in his eyes to be threatening. I don't see the Hindu reaction purely in terms of one fundamentalism pitted against another. The sense of history that the Hindus are now developing is a new thing (To prevent emotions from spilling over and creating fresh tensions), it is not enough to use that fashionable word from Europe: fascism. *Wise men should understand (the historical) and ensure that it does not remain in the hands of fanatics.* Rather they should use it for the intellectual transformation of India.[8]

Naipaul's comments could have been the beginning of an intellectual debate on the role of religion in the formation of individual and collective identity in India. However they were grabbed by political groups, circulated out of context, flashed on banners and robbed of their content. Naipaul rightly says, "you say that India has a secular character, which is historically unsound."[9] Fortunately or unfortunately, religion is a part and parcel of every Indian's identity. And this is not a recent development. Right from the earliest years of independence, our election campaigns have been won or lost on issues as diverse as cow slaughter, Muslim personal law and building of temples. The time has come for Indian intellectuals to accept the un-secular character of secular India. Naipaul's stand could have been the beginning of an intellectual debate in India and could have kept the new born sense of the self from passing into the hands of the fanatics. Unfortunately, the movement was left to be twisted and turned to suit vested political interests. Naipaul's works and his commitment to India calls for opening up those debates that have so far been forced under the garb of secularism. This calls for action on the part of the intellectuals, in the absence of which, such movements degenerate into fanaticism.

4
Questions of Marginality

> What the mutinies were also helping to define was the strength of the general intellectual life, and the wholeness and humanism of the values to which all Indians now felt they could appeal. And—strange irony—the mutinies were not to be wished away. They were part of the beginning of a new way for many millions, part of India's growth, part of its restoration.
>
> V.S. Naipaul, *India: A Million Mutinies Now.*

India: A Million Mutinies Now stands closest to the idea of homecoming for Naipaul. It marks Naipaul's surfacing after a long quest amongst the now diminishing ripples of socio-political-cultural paradoxes of India. He sees a million mutinies breaking out in the margins: mutinies of castes, of class, and of gender. He sees these rebellions as positive movements towards the restoration of India. Naipaul observes that the dark shrouds, holding beneath them centuries of violence are being torn apart; structures of dominance are being dismantled. Naipaul finds India in its offices, kitchens, galleries and chawls; in Dalit rebellions and in women's movements. In the very same sights that had shocked him into a rage in *An Area of Darkness* he now sees positive movement. He sees wounded India's dark festering bandages being torn apart by these mutinious people in the margins. He sees these as empowering symbols and with their coming to the centre, he sees India on its way to being whole again.

This change in vision marks a great shift from Naipaul's first perceptions recorded in *An Area of Darkness* and in *India: A Wounded Civilization.* It brings into question the factors that go into the formation of a writer's perspective. Naipaul himself explains the process—sometimes in direct sentences and sometimes in his very manner of documenting facts. This discussion begins with the last chapter in the book, 'The House on the Lake: A Return to India' with the specific purpose of establishing a link between *An Area of Darkness* and *India: A Million Mutinies Now*. Although placed twenty-seven years apart in time, both books are commentaries on each other and provide explicit examples of the diasporic forces at work within the writer, of which he is himself unaware. I cite a few examples:

> What I hadn't understood in 1962, or had taken too much for granted, was the extent to which the country had been remade...restored to itself.... (*MM* 517)
>
> I had carried in my bones that idea of abjectness and defeat and shame. It was the idea I had taken to India on that slow journey by train and ship in 1962; it was the source of my nerves. (*MM* 517)
>
> In 27 years I had succeeded in making a kind of return journey, shedding my Indian nerves, abolishing the darkness that separated me from my ancestral past. (*MM* 516)
>
> The India I had gone to in 1962 was like a different country. (*MM* 490)
>
> The India of my fantasy and heart was something lost and irrecoverable. The physical country existed. I could travel to that; I had always wanted to. But on that first journey I was a fearful traveller. (*MM* 419)

These stand in contrast to the personal insights scattered all over *An Area of Darkness*:

> The physique of Europe had melted away.... Men had been diminished and deformed; they begged and whined. Hysteria had been my reaction.... It mattered little through whose eyes I was seeing the East; there had as yet been no time for this type of self-assessment. (*AD* 13)
>
> Superficial impressions, intemperate reactions. (*AD* 13)

> ...the reawakening within India of disputes about language, religion, caste and region. India, it seems, will never cease to require the arbitration of a conqueror...this absence of growth and development...only a series of beginnings, no final creation. (*AD* 202)

> In a year I had not learned acceptance. I had learned my separateness from India.... (*AD* 252)

> Ten months later I was to revisit Bombay and to wonder at my hysteria.... It was my eye that had changed. (*AD* 45)

It is evident that Naipaul has written about something more than India. He has also written about himself in the process. The line of demarcation between the two subjects that Naipaul the writer deals with is very thin and one cannot entirely agree with Anniah Gowda that Naipaul is only "writing about himself, not India."[1] Nor can one agree with William Walsh when he credits Naipaul for his "needle like precision" and "literary acupuncture"[2] Naipaul's arena is a dappled area of the separate working of his double vision (external and internal). *India: A Million Mutinies Now* is a book in which Naipaul has been able to create a pattern out of his double vision. The book strikes a wonderful balance between the interiority of Naipaul's experience and the external experiences that he encounters and observes. The book is divided into nine chapters and each chapter is a profusion of characters and voices, which speak for themselves.

The first chapter 'Bombay Theatre' discusses the lives of eleven people from different walks of life, their families and acquaintances, their loyalties and prejudices. But before that, it records, in Naipaul's own words, the factors that had governed his reactions to India in 1962. This, in a way, provides a prelude to the entirely different way in which Naipaul records his reactions in the pages that follow. Papu is a twenty-nine year old Jain stockbroker, a mild mannered and God fearing person who has been doing very well professionally. The pattern of growth is drawn out—he "had made more money in the last five years than his father had made in all his working life" (*MM* 9). Unlike his father, he had received formal education. He recognised his lack of the "killer instinct" in business and had thus moved to those business areas to which he was temperamentally more suited.

He suffered periods of anxiety regarding the predicament of the mild race of Jain businessmen in face of aggressive business tactics adopted by others. He was also deeply concerned about social welfare and wanted to devote most of his time to it. However, he was also aware that he could invest more money in social welfare by working harder in his profession rather than by working in the slums. Papu had devised his own programme of striking a balance between his job and his devotion to social work. His idea of social work was also very different from that of the older generation of Jains. Instead of building marble temples, he believed in building orphanages and hospitals. He used the latest expertise in his work but was very deeply rooted in his religious beliefs. Papu is thus presented as a representative of positive growth in the conventional Indian business world. Through Papu, one also gets a glimpse of the ways of functioning of other business houses like Tata, Birla, Bajaj and Ambani.

Mr. Patil is a Shiv Sena 'area leader.' His father had worked for forty years in the tool-room of a factory and was so weighed down by family responsibilities that he had no idea of the activities of the Shiv Sena. Mr. Patil was brought up comfortably and this gave him security and an idea of his social concerns. He joined the Shiv Sena and steadily worked for the people in his 'area.' But there was a paradox in the way Mr. Patil looked at things: he was deeply concerned about the deprivation of Maharashtrians brought about by non-Maharashtrians but he had absolutely no sympathy for the Dalit organizations. He believed that they hadn't suffered much and their activism was mainly political. His antipathy towards Muslims verged on hatred but he had no qualms about "exporting man power to Dubai and the Middle East" for a living (22). Although Mr. Patel's *atma-vishwas* was his cherished gift from Ganpati, he was reluctant to recognize the same *atma-vishwas* in Dalits.

In Mr. Patil, one finds the earliest beginnings of the recognition of the 'self.' His idea of 'self' and self-confidence is muddled up and biased but it is a kind of beginning. This was absent in his father's generation when the main concern was the day-to-day needs of the family. In Mr. Patil's generation, the concerns had broadened from the personal to the social sphere but this had also brought with it a lot of confusion typical to societies passing through change.

Anwar is an educated and sensitive young man caught between his Muslim faith and its degeneration into violence. He had absolute faith in Islam and its concept of brotherhood. He believed that the world could be set right through the teachings of Islam and lack of education was the main cause behind young Muslims slipping into crime and violence. He recognized the hopeless situation of the crime infested area where he lived but could not ever think of leaving that area for a better life elsewhere. His thoughts were not of personal progress but of the progress of the community. The very fact that he had been able to preserve his sensitivity and his reason in spite of living amidst group fights and murders was a sign of change. Anwar's grandfather had died at forty, his father was happy to have crossed sixty-four. This too, spoke of the better life that had come to the people.

Mr. Raote had been one of the first eighteen recruits of the Shiv Sena and was now the chairman of the standing committee of the Bombay Corporation. His father had worked as a mechanic in All India Radio and had educated all his children. Mr. Raote's first ambition was to join the military. He couldn't get into the military; he couldn't do a course in engineering, as his father couldn't afford the expense. So he took up a job as a clerk in the Corporation while his father worked as a carpenter in a film studio to enable his sister to become a doctor. His marriage was a "love-match" and thus was followed by more financial burdens. He found an opening in furniture work and his designs found favour all over Bombay. From furniture, he moved to the building business and had been doing very well ever since. His dedication to the Sena and its work had continued all along. In his business he had worked "to accommodate the middle-class Maharashtrian" (52). His front door had no latch, it was always open. He was deeply religious and his religion was an extension of his courage and confidence which branched off into his social concerns:

> The worldly man who wanted to be an officer and an engineer, the Sena worker, the devout Hindu: there were three layers to him, making for a chain of belief and action. (53)

Papu worked in Dharavi, feeding around five hundred people every Sunday. But his idea of service was to help people help themselves. Charity for the sake of charity had no value. It was no longer the old Hindu idea of charity as an automatic act to earn divine goodwill for oneself. It was now strongly linked to social concern.

Mr. Ghate was also a Sena official. His father had been a millworker and his family "had never owned a book" till he went to college (62). In contrast to Mr. Patil and Mr. Raote, Mr. Ghate was not at all religious. Although he could afford better accommodation, he continued to live in a chawl because both he and his wife were used to the chawl life. His wife had had serious problems coping with the solitude of the staff quarters. "*Absence of civic sense*" was the most difficult problem and he believed that one had to start with the children to rectify this malady among the chawl dwellers (65). Mr. Ghate had progressed much as compared to his mill-worker father. This progress had given him new ideas, about himself and about others. These ideas were sometimes in conflict with each other but Mr. Ghate carried on, anchored by Sena pride.

On the other side of Sena monopoly was the criminal world of Bombay. The businessmen and politicians used professional criminals to get their work done:

> to deter political defections, to encourage political donations; to enforce payment of a debt, to compel adherence to an unwritten 'black-money' contract. (69)

Having turned criminals, these people had fallen out of the mainstream and now there was no hope of return. With criminal records against their names they were doomed to spend the rest of their lives in the underworld. Here too, the religious faith had somehow survived. How they explained their actions in the light of their deep faith in religion was a paradox. Living in the shadow of death, cut off from society, these people held on to whatever faith their deities inspired in them in spite of knowing that they were doomed.

> The gangsters at the top...the dons...could be courted by political parties and film people.... But the men below, the men in the middle...were doomed. (75)

Religion had a special place in a society that was passing through the stress and strain of change and pujaris were much in demand. In Bombay, with its paradoxes and its divisions of faith, the pujaris were as much in demand as the Sena men.

The "Electric pujari" customized religious ceremonies and offered recorded pujas on tape; the other pujari who has been dealt in detail in the text was satisfied with whatever he earned and conducted pujas in the traditional way. This variety appealed to the people of Bombay for whom the very concept of religion and puja was undergoing change. Nandini worked as a journalist and did not believe in ritualistic puja, but the pujari was called by her family on auspicious occasions. The pujari had a much more comfortable life in Bombay than what he could have had in his native village.

Subroto had come to Bombay from Calcutta. He was lucky to have adjusted to his work in the art department of an advertising agency. His friend, the film writer, had not been so lucky. His story was a story of defeat. He could not work in accordance with the current demands of the film directors. His loyalty to his art made him pay a very heavy price. He not only lost his work, but lost out on goodwill as well. He continued with whatever screen-writing he was offered and kept on drifting back to Calcutta:

> Calcutta is where I studied. I keep on drifting back. It's my home town, mentally. It's where I feel comfortable. That's where I feel things are happening all the time, and

> that's where I acquired the ambition of being a film writer. (85)

The Bengali film writer was one of those millions who drifted across the metropolis, those who could not be rooted.

Namdeo Dhasal and his wife Mallika represent another layer of society where there has been considerable movement. Namdeo Dhasal was the founder of the Dalit Panthers and was also known for the poetry that he wrote. His political career had seen many ups and downs but he was not much bothered about that. Initially, his political failure had caused him to fall ill but he recovered. His poetry spoke of raw pain. His wife Mallika was the daughter of communist folk singers. Her mother was a high caste Hindu and father a Muslim. Mallika and Namdeo's marriage was a marriage of the minds which faltered on ground realities. The outcome was Mallika's autobiography, *I Want to Destroy Myself*. Namdeo had come a long way from being an outcaste Dalit in his native village. He drew inspiration from Ambedkar and thus created an identity for himself and for others. He worked for the prostitutes and other oppressed classes of people. He had himself lived through much oppression as a young Mahar caste boy in his village, as a taxi driver in Bombay, and as a resident of the "Dhor slum." Therefore he was full of anger. It was his exposure to Ambedkar's movement that made him channelize his anger into a positive political force.

This assertion of the self was the beginning of the dismantling of old prejudices that required some men to be lower than others. It was a way of growth for thousands of marginalized people. With the coming of education and equal job opportunities a beginning had been made, but it was a political movement like Namdeo's that gave people an identity which they could be comfortable with, and even proud of. The first section 'Bombay Theatre' ends with Namdeo's story. Naipaul has presented a cross-section of life in metropolitan Bombay. Each nook and corner, each one-roomed chawl is closely observed. The chapter depicts a metropolis undergoing great change. The movement shows in occasional ruptures of the social fabric and in the somewhat paradoxical values of people.

'The Secretary's Tale' is the story of Rajan, his father and his grandfather. It is a story of how people's idea of themselves changes with the passage of time. Rajan's grandfather was a petty official in one of the law courts near Tanjore. He got into a fight with a British officer and had no option but to leave. He came to Calcutta with his family. There he trained his son to be a stenographer. The stenographer son rose to great heights and lived in style. In the 1946 Hindu-Muslim riots in Calcutta he lost everything. Young Rajan was brought up by his step-sister. He too, began his career as a typist but struggled all along for a more creative job. After a number of jobs with various firms in different capacities, Rajan too became a secretary with a firm in Bombay. He felt he had a lot more talent and creativity that could have been put to better use but he lived with a sense of fulfilment at having been able to take care of all his responsibilities:

> I haven't risen beyond what my father and grandfather could rise to, at the beginning of the century. The only consolation is that, even as a secretary, I am not as badly off as most other secretaries are. And perhaps, even, I no longer believe I am just a secretary. (135)

'Breaking Out' observes the layers of change that had come to the southern parts of India over a period of three generations. It begins with observations on Goa; its Portuguese past had nearly wiped out the old India. With the Portuguese occupation of Goa, the conquest of Vijaynagar and the rise of Mughal power in the North, Hindu India had very slim chances of survival. But Hindu India survived:

> Through all the twists and turns of history, through all the imperial venturings in this part of the world, which that Portuguese arrival in India portended, and finally through the unlikely British presence in India, a Hindu India had grown again, more complete and unified than any India in the past. (143)

'Breaking Out' is mainly about how the old Hindu-Brahmin India survived and turned itself into an agent of growth and development in new India. Deviah, a science reporter for a newspaper, went on a pilgrimage to the shrine of Ayappa every year. He was also well versed in the story of Ayappa and the mythological details it contained.

Dr. Srinivasan, chairman of the Atomic Energy Commission came from a family of priests. His grandfather had been a *Purohit* and was only a matriculate. He wanted his son to pass the university examination and so the son went to the university. However, Sanskrit lessons continued at home and the son was taught all the religions rituals. In 1925, the son, Dr. Srinivasan's father, joined the education department and became a teacher. The new education and the Brahmin training stayed together in him. These were the forces that created Dr. Srinivasan. Naipaul sees this as a kind of continuity of old learning:

> The old Hindu-Sanskrit learning—which a late 18th century scholar-administrator like Sir William Jones had seen as archaic...that old learning had, 200 years later, in the most roundabout way, seeded the new. (152)

Subramaniam, also a scientist, came from a similar Hindu-Brahmin background. His grandfather understood that knowledge of English was essential. He could not do much about his own education but he sent his son to an English medium school. This son went to the university and later worked with a leading scientist of those times. With knowledge of modern science, there occurred a change in sensibility. There was a conflict between science and the rituals he practised at home. He rejected caste prejudices and rituals. The concept of puja also changed. He started writing books on science in the local language. Into this family was born Subramaniam. Subramaniam could look at a century of change within his family in a very analytical manner. He saw the predominance of Brahmins on the Indian science scene as a "development of history" and although he credited the old Hindu Brahmin tradition of pursuit of knowledge for this development, he was also aware that Brahmins were "responsible still for many things on our social landscape" (160-61).

Pravas came from a priestly family of the East. His grandfather was a priest, his father had retired as a government clerk. His grandfather had lived in a secure world as purohit to a royal family; his religion was his profession. For Pravas's father the security of the old world was replaced. His job with the government gave him his livelihood. The puja, the rituals and the chanting of mantras became a part of his personal world. He read religious texts and tried to interpret them. He also read modern philosophical works in English, Devnagri and Bengali. He had received the Gandhian philosophy. All this brought about a change in him. His attitude towards rituals, food and dress-related rules changed. In his son, Pravas, these were further modified:

> I have made one more level of transformation than my father did from his father's time. I am more liberal in outlook than my father. I've probably become more questioning.... My father got a part of what his father had, and I have only a part of the rituals my father had. (167-68)

Kala's story is also one of progress. She "did the publicity for a big organization" (171). She was in her twenties and single. Her grandfather had started from nothing and had gone on to become an administrator in a princely-state. Her mother studied up to class ten and was married. This marriage distorted her life and neither she nor her parents could do anything about it. That is why she brought up Kala to be financially independent. Thus ideas and ideologies changed over a period of three generations and the potential that was neglected in Kala's mother came to be recognized and valued in Kala.

Prakash hailed from an agricultural family of Bellary and was a minister in the non-Congress state government of Karnataka. He was a lawyer before he entered politics. He spoke of the power that the politicians wielded and the chaos created due to the transition caused by industrialization and the green revolution:

> During this transition period, we are slowly cutting from the moral ethos of our grandfathers, and at the same time, we don't have the westerner's idea of discipline

> and social justice. At the moment things are chaotic here. (189)

The pundit who worked as *mukhthesar* for the maharaja of Mysore had his own history. His grandfather worked as a cook in the palace and this grandfather sent him to the Sanskrit College in Mysore city where he studied for twenty years. At the end of his education, he was appointed *mukhthesar* by the Maharaja. He served the Maharaja even after he lost his privy purse. After the death of the Maharaja he took up a job as the manager of a marriage hall. He was now no longer the Maharaja's *mukhthesar* but a man in his own right:

> Four times a year now he went to the palace, to make offerings to the head of the royal family.... But now he didn't go as an employee or palace servant. He went as a man in his own right. (202)

The chapter 'Breaking Out' portrays people from different walks of life who had come out of the old Hindu world of their parents and grandparents and were working towards new goals, and building up a new concept of selfhood. They were thus ushering into the Indian scene a new growth and development. Working alongside were 'Little Wars.' These were movements in South India that sought to break the old order not in a gradual way but as a direct and immediate goal. It was a war between South and North, between brahmin and non-brahmin.

The movement in the south had begun with Periyar. It had given people an idea of themselves. The DMK victory in the elections was a great cause of celebration for the non-brahmins. Periyar, the man behind the cause was iconized. As years passed, breaks occurred even within the DMK. Periyar, being an atheist and a rationalist, offered the vision of a world governed by science, free of caste and religion. His war was against caste prejudice and he rejected everything that created caste distinction—be it temples or temple tanks. But his movement was indifferent to the "looting" of temples and to the "replacement of temple icons by fakes" (224). The chapter gives a detailed account of Periyar's life and ideologies and how these came to be imbibed by his followers. Entire passages are narrated by Sadanand Menon and the figure of the writer hardly surfaces. It is through Menon that the reader comes to know how the Periyar movement in the end came to stand for those very things that it had opposed in the first place:

> The anti-brahmin movement was not a movement of all the non-brahmin castes. It was a movement mainly of the middle castes.... When their government came to power, they became the oppressors. (226)

However, the Periyar movement had touched people in various ways. Gopalakrishnan turned into a rationalist at a very young age. At school he was made to realize his middle caste status that was thought fit only for "grazing cattle" (226). Gradually, Gopalakrishnan moved away from religion and found confidence in Periyar's movement and literature. He entered publishing business and published school textbooks and books about Periyar's movement.

The passion of Palani was stronger than that of Gopalakrishnan. The seed of this passion was sown when his brother was shouted at for taking water from a brahmin hotel. This sense of injustice kept building up, and when Palani came across Periyar, he found all his answers. His father was a government clerk but Palani could become an engineer because of the seats that were reserved for students from non-brahmin castes. He had Periyar to thank for this concession. From a weaver to a clerk to an engineer—the story of his family had been one of progress. This was the way in which Periyar's movement had touched so many lives, so many families.

Passion breeds passion. Kakushthan's passion was to be a pure and perfect brahmin. This passion had come to him at a very late stage in life. As a school going child he had to suffer for his Brahmin dress, for the caste-mark on his forehead and for his *churki*. He had long and heated discussions with his father but he was not allowed to adopt modern ways. He tried to run away, he tried to break away from this brahmin past but in the end he came back. His only passion in life now was to live the pure life of a brahmin. This he had done by beginning to make minor and major changes in the old brahmin lifestyle. That was the way the community could be preserved.

Veeramani was Periyar's successor, his "philosophical heir." His consistent loyalty to Periyar had earned him his position. His marriage was also arranged by Periyar to a girl from an established family so that he could take care of the party without having to worry about his livelihood. He carried on the Self-Respect movement and his own life was a story of success—financial as well as social. His father had been a tailor and now his children were all studying abroad. The anti-brahmin movement had catapulted him into glory and fame.

There was another kind of revolution that, for a short period of time, broke out like a war. This was a Maoist style revolution started by peasants belonging to the lower castes. They wanted to overthrow the government and kill the landowners. The rebellion was soon controlled by police intervention but it uncovered the failure of the Periyar movement "...Periyar had struggled against caste alone; he hadn't thought of class" (277). The people at the lowest level had been left out and the rebellion was an assertion of their existence and their need to be included in the mainstream.

The chapter records revolutions and rebellions at personal as well as public level. This unrest was the way of new beginning for the non-brahmin middle castes and the lower castes. For people like Kakusthan and Sugar, it was a struggle to maintain the purity and continuity of the old world. The struggle was on both sides, it was between the old world and the new. Both worlds changed, both adapted and continued. Only this time the continuity also spoke of a new identity among people—an assertion of their newly acquired idea of the self.

The fifth chapter 'After the Battle' focuses on eastern India and on Calcutta in particular. Like the British architecture in Calcutta, Chidananda Das Gupta was also a product of British times: "a boxwallah." Chidananda worked for ITC and had a comfortable lifestyle. But he was not comfortable with the two sides of his existence: his status and work at the ITC required him to be someone he was not and his yearning for intellectual and creative life called for a different kind of life. His association with Shantiniketan was his life force. In the end he left his job at ITC and became a film-maker and writer. Rabindranath Tagore and Satyajit Ray formed an important part of his mental makeup.

Ashok was a South Indian brahmin whose father had settled in Calcutta. He was into the marketing business. He had got into this profession with great difficulty. His generation was passing though an era of change where old values had to be weighed against new values. He rejected the traditional "bride-seeing" and opted for a self-choice marriage. His professional life was an example of regeneration on the Indian business scene. The quiet world of the boxwallah had given way to cut throat competition and marketing had begun to make tough demands on people. The Marwari businessmen had been gaining a monopoly over the major business houses, while at the other end the Bengalis were content to display their trade unionism and criticize the Marwaris. The Marwari success story in Calcutta had been fuelled by the Bengali mindset:

> ...he is indolent, he doesn't want to work...and he must protect his dignity at all costs. He will publicly despise the Marwari trader, but he wouldn't do the same job himself. (346)

Dipanjan and his wife Arati both taught in colleges. Both had been associated with the Naxalite movement in Calcutta during their college days. Their marriage had cut across caste barriers evoking much opposition from Arati's parents. They came from families that had had modern education. Arati's father was a scientist and an IES officer whereas Dipanjan's father was a Ph.D. in biochemistry and a communist. The Naxalite movement had been the passion of Dipanjan's life and when the movement met its end, Dipanjan withdrew and started pondering over what had gone wrong. What had seemed to be a wonderful beginning for millions of people in the villages seemed to have gone astray midway. Dipanjan's years in jail with other Naxalite prisoners, mainly those accused of urban violence including murders disillusioned him about the movement. He was released by the Government and he went to London to study Physics. On his return, he chose to teach in an obscure college and avoided meeting his friends from earlier days. The story of Dipanjan and Arati is that of a generation led astray by ideas. It was a generation whose ideas for reform were its undoing.

Debu, who held a high position as an executive, had been associated with the Naxalite movement in its earliest stages but had later developed ideological differences with the leadership. He had his own clear-cut idea about the reason behind the failure of the movement. Debu had been closely involved with the beginnings of the Naxalite movement and had actually believed in its success. He had even tried to reason out Charu Mazumdar's policy of individual killing. Later he fell out with Charu Mazumdar and went underground in April 1970.

Debu's major concern was with the idea of development in India. He was pained by the intellectual decay and the economic crisis of India, especially the sufferings of the poor. He still believed in the revolution and was convinced that a revolution could set things right here and now. Earlier Debu had been pained when, during his lectures on India in America, he had been asked—"How come you're starving and begging for food, if you're so great?" (334). This had led to his joining the radical communist wing. Years after the failure of the Naxalite movement, he still believed in revolution:

> The only change—a big change—between then and now is that at that time, in the late 60s, I thought I could be a part of the revolution, and now I know that I shall be a *witness* to it. A supportive witness. I don't think the need for revolution has changed. (333)

The chapter ends with Naipaul's comments on Calcutta. With the going away of the British he sees the Anglo-Bengali intellectual life coming to an end. In the poverty of the urban poor he sees Calcutta in a state of decay. However, amidst the decay, he observes certain spots of regeneration in the cinema of Satyajit Ray and in the optimism of people like Debu. 'After the Battle' is Naipaul's documentation of the movement in the Indian social fabric that occurred in the 1960s and '70s. This movement marks intellectual confusion of the times when the old ideologies were set aside and a search was on for a new set of ideologies to live by. This coupled with economic crisis accentuated the confusion of those times.

The sixth chapter 'The End of the Line' contains the response of Indian Muslims to the partition of India. Naipaul begins with a discussion of Satyajit Ray's film, *The Chess Players.* Naipaul uses the film to comment on the decadent Muslim power in the nineteenth century and the annexation of Oude, which stalled Muslim India:

> Lucknow was the end of the line for Muslim India.... In its historical heart it is like a graveyard from the days of the Nawabs of Oude, full of the ruins of war. The city was shelled and fought over during the Mutiny; afterwards the British preserved the ruins as a memorial, and passed them on to independent India. (351-52)

Naipaul meets Rashid, who, even after one hundred and thirty years, carries the scar of defeat at the hands of the British. Many middle-class Muslims had left for Pakistan and all that remained in Lucknow, once known as the epitome of Muslim culture, were people who were "vulnerable, withdrawn and highly strung" (354). With Rashid, Naipaul walks down the market and finds the practitioners of ancient crafts in a state of decadence. The embroiderers, the silver-foil makers, lived a life of squalor:

> All the jobs here have this soul-destroying quality. They are doing it only because their fathers did it before them. (360)

Rashid came from an old Shia Muslim family. His father had a successful photography business. His shops sold cameras and photographic equipment. This was in 1911. After independence, in 1947, Rashid's father wanted to shift to Pakistan along with his business. His own nephew who transferred the shop in his own name cheated him. Rashid's father stayed in India but decided to marry his daughter to a Pakistani Muslim. Rashid got his education at La Martinière and grew up with two cultures: the secular culture at school and the religious culture at home. After his father's death, Rashid drifted in various ways. He went to England and worked in a Kentucky Fried Chicken shop. He went to Pakistan. But even Pakistan was disillusionment. Rashid could not belong to the aggressive business minded world of Indian Muslims in Pakistan. He felt stifled by the Islamic laws that had total monopoly over an individual's life. He returned to India for the scant sense of belonging it still had to offer.

Amir came from an aristocratic Muslim family. His father was a Raja. He wished to instill in his son the truest values of Islam. At the same time he wanted his son to have a modern education. Like Rashid, Amir also grew up with two cultures. His father's oscillations between India, Pakistan, Iran and England kept him from being rooted. When his father declared his intention of accepting Pakistani citizenship the family suffered hardships in India. His father's failure to be integrated into the mainstream in Pakistan caused deeper confusion in Amir. His cultural upbringing and his study of astronomy complicated this confusion:

> His political and religious passions had bequeathed many languages, many cultures, many modes of thought and emotion to his son. He had had his son's ears pierced, to pledge him to the service of the faith.... But with that—his academic work in Cambridge and London had been in astronomy—Amir had also developed religious doubts. (380)

Naipaul notes the violence caused to the Muslim psyche as a result of the partition of India. The Muslims, so far rooted in India were doubly displaced. In India, they strove to get away to a place that promised to reinstate their pride and position as rulers. In Pakistan they could not be integrated into the mainstream and were marginalized as *mohajirs.*

This double exclusion is crystallized in Rashid's concluding remark:

> That sense of belonging, which I had in India, I knew I couldn't find anywhere else. Yet I also know that I can never be a complete person now. I can't ignore partition. It's a part of me. I feel rudderless.... The creation and existence of Pakistan has damaged a part of my psyche. I simply cannot pretend it doesn't exit. I can't pretend that life goes on.... (387)

Amidst the grim darkness of the worlds of Rashid and Amir, Naipaul discovers a small ray of hope. This ray of hope is Parveen, who represents those Muslims who have been integrated into the Indian social fabric, those Muslims who cherish no religious or cultural yearnings for Pakistan. Parveen came from a family of landlords and lawyers and had entered active politics. She saw herself as Indian and blamed the Muslim unrest in India to ignorance and a lack of proper education and ignorance.

The chapter on one hand discusses in finest detail the genesis and nature of the problem of alienation of Muslims in India. On the other hand, it also discusses the ways in which integration can be made possible. Naipaul's scale tilts heavily towards the gloomy despair of Rashid and Amir. But Parveen stands as a ray of hope. And with her stands the hope of the millions. Naipaul leaves the possibility open to Parveen. The chapter carries no concluding remarks from Naipaul.

The seventh chapter, 'Women's Era' shows the change that had come to the Indian woman's idea of herself and the role played by Vishwa Nath. Naipaul begins with his own difficulties with Russell's *Diary*. Through his own example and Rashid's, Naipaul lays the groundwork for individual responses to literary work. On this groundwork he builds the Indian women's response to the women's magazines in India. He sees these magazines as being structured around the psychological needs of a changing population. Vishwa Nath, the editor of *Women's Era* was as iconoclast and a conventional man rolled into one. Through *Women's Era, Femina, Savvy* and *Eve's Weekly* Naipaul sees different kinds of women, with different sets of priorities and values. The paradox of Vishwa Nath's mind was the paradox of a vast majority of Indian women who were just entering the outside world for the first time. Therefore Vishwa Nath's became the most popular women's magazine.

The striking note in the chapter is the gradual change in Naipaul's opinion of *Women's Era.* He lays out the whole process. Initially, he found *Women's Era* to be dull. The articles were in fact general instructions on the desired code of behaviour on social occasions or on health and fitness of the family. Later, Naipaul looks at its target audience and tries to place the magazine in the indispensable informative role it played for its target audience. In this way Naipaul learns to look at the magazine with a new sense of admiration. Naipaul, in *India: A Million Mutinies Now,* adopts this method throughout. The chapter 'Women's Era' shows the clearest working of Naipaul's new method. The chapter in a way summarizes the change in Naipaul's perspective from *An Area of Darkness* to *India: A Million Mutinies Now.* He begins with a rejection of *Women's Era,* goes on to analyse the magazine, its editor, and its target readers. He then arrives at a newfound admiration for the work being done by this magazine. The pattern of his coming to terms with India is replicated in his treatment of *Women's Era.*

The second last chapter, 'The Shadow of the Guru' is a detailed analysis of the psychology of Sikh insurgency in India. He sees the Sikh militancy as a part of a larger process of awakening in India:

> To awaken to history was to cease to live instinctively. It was to begin to see oneself and one's group the way the outside world saw one; and it was to know a kind of rage.... There had been a general awakening. But everyone awakened first to his own group or community... every group sought to separate its rage from the rage of others. (420)

Gurtej Singh is the main narrator in this chapter and it is through him that Naipaul explains how a realization of the

Sikh identity mutated into insurgency. The origins of the Sikh faith were in militant action against Muslim oppression. This militant streak surfaced and got lost. In an earlier chapter Naipaul had described how the Naxalite movement had gone astray from its ideals and was lost. He repeats the same about Sikh insurgency in this chapter. The reader sees the movement in its various stages through the eyes of the people involved in it. The chapter alternates such accounts with the stories of the Sikh Gurus that form a part of the collective consciousness of the people that narrate their stories.

Naipaul does not reject insurgency but sees it as a part of a larger process of change in the people's idea of themselves. Religious identity is the first step in people's idea of themselves and therefore the insurgency in Punjab started at the religious level. Naipaul has also exposed the break in the unified idea of religion that came to people like Buta Singh. The picture that emerges is that of strife as an outlet for pent up emotions of the past; militancy as a step towards the restoration of the past Sikh glory.

The last chapter is a return to India for Naipaul. In this chapter he discusses candidly the psychology behind his first impassioned rage in *An Area of Darkness*. Naipaul visits Kashmir, the hotel Liward and its inhabitants: Aziz and Mr. Butt. Naipaul sees how India has changed and how his eye had changed over the past twenty-seven years. In places where Naipaul earlier observed decay of tradition, he now saw new creative beginnings. In the confusion of the immediate period after independence, he found a new sense of organization and he saw India on the move. He saw the socio-political disturbances and the failed attempts at revolution as a part of India's growth:

> What the mutinies were also helping to define was the strength of the general intellectual life, and the wholeness and humanism of the values to which all Indians now felt they could appeal. And—strange irony—the mutinies were not to be wished away. They were a part of the beginning of a new way for many millions, part of India's growth, part of its restoration. (518)

"In 1960 I was still a colonial, travelling to far-off places..." (*FC* II). It was around this time that Naipaul was travelling in India for *An Area of Darkness.* His views on India were therefore the views of a colonial. By the time he came to *India: A Million Mutinies Now,* he had ceased to be a colonial. He had arrived at the multiple perspectives offered by post-colonial vision. He had learnt to see India as India saw itself. This brought with it a sense of healing and a sense of homecoming for Naipaul.

India: A Million Mutinies Now is Naipaul's third and final stage of the unravelling of the problematic relation between himself and India. The book recalls his earlier books on India and attempts a revision of his earlier judgments on India. The structure of *An Area of Darkness* and *India: A Million Mutinies Now* is similar. Both begin with a description of the crowds of Bombay, but the difference in tone sets them apart. While *An Area of Darkness* ends in 'Flight,' an escape from the painful reality of India, *India: A Million Mutinies Now* in its last chapter declares a 'Return to India.' In *India: A Million Mutinies Now* India is seen through the eyes of its various narrators. Naipaul, the writer, empathises with them and thus arrives at a resting place for his overwhelming diasporic concerns for India.

5

Resurgent Lives

> The new world was so new: it had begun for some with their grandfathers and for most with their fathers. And people had travelled so far so fast that many active people had a success story to tell, their own sometimes, or that of someone in their family.
>
> V.S. Naipaul, *India: A Million Mutinies Now.*

The progression in the personal circumstance of people which Naipaul observes in *India: A Million Mutinies Now* is closely linked with Naipaul's coming to terms with his diasporic status and in the process coming to terms with India. This is clearly represented in the changing perceptions of Indian women in his books on India. The portrayal of women in *An Area of Darkness* and in *India: A Wounded Civilization* is offhand and incidental. Women are shown to be a part of the decaying system. They are incapable of bringing about any major change in the world they inhabit. They are shown to have no understanding of the changing world around them. But with *India: A Million Mutinies Now* there comes a sharp change in Naipaul's perception. Women are portrayed against their socio-economic-political backgrounds and the change that has occurred through women is carefully brought out.

In *An Area of Darkness* Naipaul observes three classes of women in India: the poor, the working class and the noveau rich. The poor are represented by the prostitutes of Bombay and their servants:

> In the dim stinking corridors sat expressionless women, very old, very dirty, shrivelled almost to futility...these

> were the sweepers, the servants of the gay girls of the Bombay poor. (*AD* 47)

Another glimpse of women in the poor sections of society is in the businesslike beggarwoman on the local trains of Bombay:

> The boy is manoeuvred and propelled through the coach by the woman who weeps and whines and briskly, without acknowledgement, collects the small coins which the passengers, without looking up, hand to her. She does not pause to plead with those who don't give. (*AD* 68)

Naipaul talks of three women of the upper income group of which only one is a full-length portrayal. All that one comes to know of Boxwallah Bunty's wife is that she has European complexion and manners. Mrs. M. Mehta, the secretary of *Women's League* also remains obscure. Mrs. Mahindra, the wife of a noveau rich contractor is shown trying very hand to adopt "modern" ways. She is keen to furnish her house with "foreign" things and speaks a strange variety of English: "I am craze for foreign...just craze for foreign" (*AD* 85). She is enthusiastic about her role as a modern housewife and is enterprising in her own way. However, with the arrival of her father-in-law she quickly loses all her enthusiasm and regresses into her traditional role: "In no time at all she had dwindled into the Indian daughter-in-law. We heard little now of her craze for foreign" (*AD* 89). In *India: A Wounded Civilization* Naipaul makes repeated references to Mrs. Indira Gandhi but these are more political in content than social and hence offer no glimpse of the changes that are occurring in the social fabric of resurgent India. In rural India Naipaul meets the power-wielding Patel whose daughter-in-law is a graduate. One doesn't come to know if her education has empowered her in some way but her being a graduate has definitely added glamour to Patel's power.

> Patel...was too grand to boast of her attainments. That he could leave to others, his admirers and hangers on. And

> the others did pass on the news about the daughter-in-law of this wealthy man. She was a graduate! (*WC* 82)

> The Patel's daughter-in-law—who might not have been absolutely a graduate: she had perhaps simply gone for a few years to a secondary school—would have come from a family like the Patel's in another village. She would have exchanged one big house of grain for another.... (*WC* 87)

The Indian wife of the young foreign academic and her friend are very cursorily sketched. The wife of the foreign academic is as blind to the changes taking place in India as her husband: "Her Indian blindness to India with its roots in caste and religion was like his foreigner's easy disregard" (*WC* 117). This is replicated in the blindness of her friend towards the poor of the city she lives in:

> The women of Bombay, she said...wore a certain kind of sari...the men wore a special kind of turban. She had lived in Bombay; but already she was wrong...in Bombay the men for the most part wear trousers and shirt. (*WC* 117-18)

Helplessness and sadness that falls to the share of women is shown through the daughter of the cloth merchant who, unable to cope with the mental agony inflicted on her by her husband and in-laws commits suicide: "She suffered specially when she was not allowed to visit her sister in hospital...cyanide was detected in the viscera of the dead girl..." (*WC* 133). Irrespective of class Naipaul shows women shackled to set notions of caste and religion. Jamnadas Bajaj's rich widow who followed Gandhi is blind to all that he stood for. In spite of her loyalty to Gandhi she has not been able to break out of her idea of class and religion: "I never eat anything I haven't prepared with my own hands. Everyone knows that Moslems and Harijans have dirty habits" (*WC* 156).

Women in *An Area of Darkness* and *India: A Wounded Civilization* are shown as deeply rooted in old beliefs and customs; they are powerless against the demands of caste and society. Naipaul has shown no progression, no resurgence in his portrayal of women in *An Area of Darkness* and *India: A Wounded Civilization.* In fact, Naipaul shows them to be more retrograde than they actually were. This attitude undergoes a total change in *India: A Million Mutinies Now.* In this book Naipaul observes Indian women not as entities in isolation but as harbingers of change that has gradually come to India.

Naipaul's first statement is made on the cover jacket itself, which shows that the woman is moving and she is moving with her children. There is no one to see her off; she looks ahead as the baby suckles at her breast, waiting for the two young boys to move with her belongings. She is tired but the determination writ all over her face cannot be missed.

The picture leaves numerous questions in its wake: Where is she? What is she looking at? Where is she going? Will the boys be able to carry her belongings? What are the things she wants to carry with her? Why is she alone? The answers to all these questions form the content of this non-fiction work. The story of the woman is the fabric on which Naipaul has etched his picture gallery. He has also shown that it is this fabric that is shred when a "million mutinies" break out.

The first section titled 'Bombay Theatre' presents a cross-section of the urban middle class women in metropolitan Bombay. These women are sometimes seen, sometimes heard and sometimes felt by their very absence. Mr. Patil's and Mr. Namdeo Dhasal's mothers are elderly women whose entire existence was contained in their role of wife and mother. Mr. Patil's mother was proud of her son's achievements and did not want to intrude into any of the "serious business her son might have to deal with" (*MM* 18). Her greatest ambition was "to bring the Ganpati image home from the image-maker's with a musical band" (21). Having been able to do that she considered herself and her sons blessed. Namdeo's mother had suffered much and "had had a breakdown" (109). She moved around the house shadow-like, silent. Their journey was nearing its close and these women hadn't yet had a taste of their personhood. The second generation of women Mrs. Raote, Mrs. Ghate and their sisters-in-law are different from them. Unlike their mothers, they are educated and have chosen their own spouses. Their "love marriage" and education has given them a greater say in family matters. Mrs. Raote is a working-woman. Her sister-in-law is a doctor. Mrs. Ghate stayed at home but did not succumb to her husband's ideologies. In spite of her husband's disinterest in religion, she kept a puja-box in the kitchen. Her sister-in-law is educated, has a career, and has married for love braving much opposition. These women have begun to realize the need for financial independence. They are still docile wives and sacrificing mothers but they have begun to explore themselves. Mrs. Ghate's puja-box bears testimony to that.

Mallika represents the third generation woman. Mallika knows herself, her potential. She seeks and expects more from marriage than what Mr. Patil's mother or Mrs. Raote ever did. She is a poet and she marries the poet in Namdev. She marries him because he called her "comrade" and he gave her the "red salaam" (105). She never could fit into the role of the shock absorber that Namdev assigned to her after their marriage. She thinks and she writes what she thinks. Her autobiography, *I Want to Destroy Myself* screams: "Male ego is the most hideous thing in our present society. Women find quite a pleasure in boosting it.... I do not believe that for anybody called Namdeo I should surrender my entire life" (109). Her conflict arises out of the clash between her clear perception of the failure of her marriage and her love for Namdeo. Her "obsession with the man and his poetry and his cause" had made her lose her freedom (109). Like so many women caught in similar situations, Mallika will not be able to make a choice between love and freedom. But the process of self-assertion has certainly begun. Mallika has her views on the law too and believes that "a mother should have a right to her child" (109). She is afraid that even if she leaves Namdeo, he would get the custody of their son once he was past seven. The fear of losing her son along with her love keeps her from seeking divorce. The landmark to be noted here is the realization of conflict, which was altogether absent earlier. The hope lies in Mallika's dream of bringing up the child to be a better, sensitive human being: "I don't want the child to grow up like his father—the negative aspects" (108). With Mallika's story the visit to the 'Bombay Theatre' comes to an end. The reader has viewed the contemporary Indian woman in the numerous roles that she appears in, on the stage of life.

'The Secretary's Tale' with its 'Glimpses of the Indian Century' takes a long look backward. In Rajan's story we meet his mothers. Rajan's father, a Brahmin, was a widower thrice. "He lost his first wife, and then he married a second time, so that his second wife could look after his first two children. When his second wife died, leaving in turn two or three children, he was forced by his relations to marry a third time. In those days such marriages were not difficult" (123). On his third wedding, Rajan's father was forty-three and his mother eighteen. She died eleven years later at the age of twenty-nine, her stepdaughter had nowhere to go when she was deserted by her husband. "This was in January 1948..." (126). In spite of their helplessness, these women managed to pass on to Rajan a perspective very different from that of his father. On being told at an interview that he ought not to have left Calcutta and "should have stayed at least for the rasgolla-like women there," Rajan "told off one of the interviewers" even at the risk of being rejected for the job. He felt it "too degrading to women" (131). When he married in 1985, his was a "civil marriage—no dowry, no give, no take..." (134). His wife was a simple, independent woman. In the professional sphere, Rajan says he hadn't risen beyond what his father and grandfather could rise to at the beginning of the century, but as a sensitised human being he has certainly made a huge leap across the century.

"Breaking Out" is the emergence of the Indian woman from the shackles of ignorance and suppression. It is the mapping out of the journey of her evolution. Scientist Subramaniam's grandmother "divided the world into three parts: *Raja seemay*—the Mysore State; *Kumpani seemay*—the Company's Land; and beyond these two areas was the rest of the world" (152-53). In such a world was born Kala's grandmother. Married at eleven, she wasn't very different from Subramaniam's grandmother but her daughter studied till class ten and dreamt of being a doctor. Her dreams and her taste for a more fulfilling life cost her marital happiness. She turned into a "chattel." "She had no time to herself...she could make no decisions...somebody always decided for her" (178). She bore physical and mental abuse. She was never able to break free but she taught her daughter Kala "how important education and financial independence are" (180). As a result "Kala was in a position to make her own life...she had her job; she was free to come and go" (175). Naipaul sees in Kala's story a very positive "historical progression" which she herself is not conscious of. This is true of the Indian woman too. She has been "breaking out" slowly, through generations. The possibilities available to the Indian women today could never have been dreamt of by their grandmothers. With more and more women breaking out, little wars were bound to follow (207). These wars occurred at different levels and mainly centred between the many selves of the Indian women.

The social structure that these women had broken came back to haunt them. Manyammai left her home in opposition to marriage and continued with her teacher-training course. She later married Periyar who had founded the Self-Respect campaign and campaigned, amongst other things, against the disabilities of women. She managed the campaign till her death. Mrs. Veeramani, in spite of her "traditional and demure and self-effacing" manner was a dutiful server of the Self-Respect cause (272). 'Little Wars' were also fought by menstruating women and girls who were segregated during their periods in a special room in a corner of Kakusthan's Brahmin colony. In spite of their so-called "polluting" effects, they went out to work through the "wicket gate at the back of the colony" and dared "pollute" the men's world by their presence (247). In Sugar's story we hear of middle-class Brahmin ladies who opt for jobs and stay unmarried rather than push their fathers to bankruptcy to arrange for their marriages. They do not see marriage as a goal.

Emerging 'After the Battle' is Chidananda's wife, a discerning woman who dissuades her husband from taking up an upmarket job, as it would turn them into "a different kind of people" (290). Torn between his "Jekyll and Hyde" existences, Childananda experiences deep anguish in bringing together the westernised lifestyle demanded by his job and the cultural yearnings of his soul. Finally, deeply disgusted, he says to himself what his wife had warned him of in the beginning. "What have I done to myself?" (292).

Arati, a schoolteacher, went through her battle in her family's opposition to her marriage to Dipanjan. Although she had been sympathetic to the Naxalite cause in the beginning, she thought it foolish to take the revolution to the people. "The poor in India believed in their fate...that...had set the revolution back by 40 years" (317). The position of women in England had further shaken her up: "...given the choice, she would have continued to live in England—this feeling of freedom, and recognition of her as an individual" (317-18). Another product of 'Little Wars' is Ashok who found the matrimonial preliminaries of "bride-seeing" humiliating and very disturbing. He was troubled as "the girl apparently had no say in the matter...everybody was waiting.... On these occasions it's all weighted in favour of the boy, and the girl's family occupies the inferior position" (330). He said no to the process. Later, he found solace in a self-choice marriage. At the 'End of the Line' we have in Parveen, the Indian woman breaking through the power structures. Optimistic, upright and confident with her ambition of entering "secular" politics, she knows exactly where she is going (363).

'Woman's Era' begins with Naipaul's first encounter with Russell's *Diary* and the different griefs it inspired in Rashid and in him. It questions the authenticity of documented history that assumes without question a sequence of events "built around the ascendancy of men."[1] This is Naipaul's prelude to a chapter, which deals with the life of Indian women and its projection in various women's magazines. In his meetings with the editors of women's magazines he discovers the tough life of the urban lower-middle class earning women members of a family:

> ...she's up at the crack of dawn...to fill the water for the day...does the morning chores, filling the tiffin-carriers for husband and children after giving them tea, breakfast...then she is off to work herself. A very long train journey.... She hardly gets a seat... She gets off from her office at 5.30 or six.... Before getting to the bus or station she would buy her vegetables or whatever she

> needs.... Then the dinner, then a bit of the children's homework.... Then she has to think of the water again. (405-06)

Naipaul's encounters with *Femina, Eve's Weekly, Savvy,* and *Women's Era* lead him to the same question with which he began. Who writes for whom? And with what authority? Are these magazines actually addressing the women? Who is their target audience? Here once again, Naipaul comes across the extreme heterogeneity within womanhood. "*Femina* is for the older woman. *Savvy* is for the city bred woman, from eighteen to thirty" (408). *Eve's Weekly* is unconventional in its outlook as compared to *Women's Era.* If readership is any indicator of effective communication *Women's Era* with its highest readership tops the list. Its editor is Vishwa Nath—a man who holds iconoclastic views on religion but is strangely conventional, even stereotyped in his concern for the role of the woman in the family. Probably the ambiguity of the editor's personality struck a concordant note with the doubts and confusions of women just emerging from their shells. What to hold on to? What to let go? What to strive for? What to fight against?—Plagued by these questions and caught in the whirlwind of change, taking cautious little steps, these women found comfort in *Women's Era* because it "did not intimidate its readers...it acknowledged the conditions in which its readers lived; and it never went beyond those conditions...with that recognition, there was always reassurance" (411). It told its readers how to conduct themselves at formal dinners, how to write a letter, how to entertain guests and all this in a tone that was "one of concern, almost love" (412). The paradox regarding women and their world which can be easily understood as coming from a male editor trapped in his own ambiguous vision was well accepted by women caught within similar visions of themselves and their worlds. "Offering instruction and reassurance, and a subtle transformation of the hard real world, to women just emerging, women whose lives were a tissue of ritual and given relationships, and didn't want to rebel or dream" (419). It gave them an honest woman's view of herself and so women could easily relate with it.

It is from here that women had started acknowledging their existence and had begun to expand their 'space.' It is from here that they later dared to rebel and dared to dream. It is in its wings that a thousand Nandinis and Kalas still wait to make their entries. What Naipaul says of India is also true of the Indian women. If the "twentieth century restoration of India to itself had taken time," it would take time for women to be restored to themselves. The transition cannot be a very smooth one. Kala's mothers will have to go through oppression, Mallikas will have to be stifled before there can emerge a Kala. The harrowing experiences of womanhood and the struggle are not to be "wished away.... They were a part of the beginning of a new way for many millions, part of India's growth, part of its restoration" (518).

This brings Naipaul to the end of his book and as the reader closes its cover, one knows the answers to all those questions, which had struck one in the beginning. The woman on the cover is the Indian woman just emerging from her grandmother's role, looking at nothing, looking through everything, looking within herself for reassurance. She is travelling to get her personhood. The boys, her children, will carry her belongings: like Ashok and Kala. Mallika's son at her breast will not grow up to be like his father. The woman is alone because she has to make this journey herself. No one else can make it for her. It reminds us of Emma Goldman's words, from *The Tragedy of Woman's Emancipation*:

> History tells us that every oppressed class gained true liberation from its masters through its own efforts. It is necessary that woman learn that lesson.... It is far more important for her to begin with her inner regeneration, to cut loose from the weight of prejudices, traditions, customs. The demand for equal rights in every vocation of life is just and fair; but, after all the most vital right is the right to love and be loved.[2]

Women may "accept the call to liberation through...activity, but loving, or getting oneself loved may be the very thing that stands in the way of acting against tradition and custom and the prejudices of those" they love.[3] This also brings us face to face with the subject-object ambiguity of women. In determining the position of women as the subject of discourse one needs to keep in mind that we are all different persons in relation to the various people in our lives. The subjectivity of women is constantly in flux. As Kristeva says:

> We are no doubt permanent subjects of a language that holds us in its power. But we are subjects *in process*, ceaselessly losing our identity, destabilized by fluctuations in our relations with the other to whom we nevertheless remain bound in a kind of homeostatis.[4]

The very identity of women is determined by a society's changing attitude towards sexuality, which is in turn socially and politically constructed. The Indian woman is constructed by discourse but she is not a "passive recipient" of discourse.[5] She is an amalgamation of a collaborator, generator, receptor and dissident within the socio-economic-political structures of dominance.

Naipaul has perceived Indian women negotiating change in their situation. He has presented them in relation to the individual capacities within which women have begun to act. A woman who may appear totally powerless as a part of the entire social set up is not so at all places and at all times. Naipaul has presented her in those spaces, in those personal capacities from where she has begun to subjectify herself. She is shown as working towards her own empowerment. In some cases the woman acts but does not speak: as in the case of Rajan's mothers and sister. In other cases she speaks but does not act: as it is with Mallika. Naipaul has effectively uncovered the tremendous potential of women, which may not show up explicitly to the undiscerning eye accustomed to surface analysis. The Indian woman is moving towards change. This movement has begun within the family which is the space most intimately known to women. It is from here that she has begun to challenge all structures of dominance. It is from here that she has begun to enlarge her space. We have to only give her time.

6

The Evolving Technique

> I would have liked to begin at the very beginning, with the blankness and anxiety of arrival. But it didn't work as narrative. And narrative was my aim. Within that, my travelling method was intended to be transparent. The reader will see how the material was gathered; he will also see how the material could have served fiction or political journalism or a travelogue. But the material here serves itself alone.
>
> V.S. Naipaul, *Finding The Centre.*

V.S. Naipaul has emerged as a leading exponent of the non-fiction novel. Naipaul first used this form in *The Middle Passage* and has, over the years perfected it to serve as a vehicle for his narrative. Naipaul's choice of the non-fiction narrative mode and his gradual shift from fiction to non-fiction is closely linked to his world vision. The non-fiction narrative mode gives him the freedom to project multiple perspectives and opposing visions. It also enables Naipaul to present those difficult strands of response that constitute our present day reality. As Naipaul progressed towards his meditations on our world, he gradually shifted from fiction to non-fiction.

The basic method adopted by an exponent of non-fiction technique is similar to that of journalism. But the function of a writer of non-fiction is very different from that of a journalist. The non-fiction writer makes use of journalistic techniques in order to fashion a first person narrative through which he expresses his ideas and meditations on a given situation. The writer emerges as a philosopher-thinker who records the present day world. Another unique feature of the non-fiction novel is its reliance on historical material, on memory and on experience. The writer delves deep into these sources and comes up with experiences that build up on each other to form the narrative of the non-fiction novel. However, the non-fiction novel does not draw on obvious data collection. Each experience is deeply drawn out and placed close to each other so that there emerges a kind of unity. Facts are quickly transformed into links in the chain of memory and experience.

This chapter attempts to study the non-fiction narrative technique as it emerges in Naipaul's three books on India: *An Area of Darkness, India: A Wounded Civilization* and *India: A Million Mutinies Now.* A parallel is drawn between Naipaul's growing understanding of the Indian fabric and its corresponding reflection in his technique. A close study of the text is made in terms of dialogue, descriptive passages and narrative passages. There are two closely woven strands in the narrative that run through these three books. These are: Naipaul's personal response to the Indian situation, and his documentation of fact and circumstance. Both these strands in the narrative spring from memory and experience which in turn are drawn from two living documents of human existence: history and literature. Apart from this, Naipaul has also attempted to give a unified form to the narrative by laying down a proper framework in terms of carefully structured chapters.

The treatment of history in *An Area of Darkness* is circumstantial. Naipaul begins with the Indian community in Trinidad which had passed into history as he grew up. In India, he meditates on the history of the Kashmir valley before the coming of the Mughal conquerors. He uses this to point at the lack of historical sense in the present day populace, who have no memory of their history before the conquests. In Shimla, he dwells on the British rule and the culture that it imparted to the people. In the South, he contemplates on the ruins of Vijaynagar and sees the death of ancient India. In *India: A Wounded Civilization* Naipaul dwells at great length on the history of India. Through history, he attempts to locate the cause behind India's problems that he had outlined in *An Area of Darkness.* The book discusses the history of Vijayanagar kingdom and the history of Maratha warfare led by Shivaji against the Mughal empire. From these two analyses, Naipaul carefully traces the present day predicament of Indian society and politics. As compared to the social and political history used in the first two books on India, Naipaul's use of history in his third book, *India: A Million Mutinies Now* is very different. Here, stress is on personal and family history: histories of individuals within the matrices of social and political change. So, the book is full of the lives and times of grandparents and parents. This analysis of personal history of individuals builds up to give a clear and detailed picture of social change.

The use of literature in the three books discussed above forms the other strand of the narrative. *An Area of Darkness* discusses Manohar Malgonkar's *The Prince* to forward Naipaul's thesis of the role of "degree" in India. Then there are brief references to the *Gita* and *Kama Sutra.* Rudyard Kipling, E.M. Forster, Jane Austen, Charles Dickens and William Hazlitt are discussed to differentiate between the European and the Indian sensibility. On the Indian side, Sri Aurobindo, Rabindranath Tagore, Jawaharlal Nehru and Nirad C. Chaudhuri are discussed.

India: A Wounded Civilization has nearly half of its first and second chapters devoted to two novels by R.K. Narayan: *Mr. Sampath* and *The Vendor of Sweets.* These two novels explain the 'Old Equilibrium' and the 'Shattering World.' U.R. Anantamurti's *Samskara* is used to draw out Naipaul's analysis of the role of *karma* in shaping the Indian sensibility. The book discusses the life, writings and ideologies of Mahatma Gandhi in great detail. In keeping with its use of personal histories of individuals, *India: A Million Mutinies Now* does not rely heavily on any major literary work of the past. Contemporary writing in terms of magazine content builds up the body of literature used in this book. Apart from the gradual change in the use of literature and history as the warp and weft of narration, Naipaul has also made a gradual change in his style of narration from *An Area of Darkness* to *India: A Million Mutinies Now.* The change is analysed in terms of dialogue, descriptive passages and narrative passages.

The use of dialogue in *An Area of Darkness* is very restricted. The lines are short and terse. Dialogues are very few and are invariably followed by long narrative passages:

> 'Open. But Why?'
> 'Isn't that the law?'
> 'Hide them.'
> 'The Metaxas is too tall to hide.'
> 'Put it flat.'
> 'I don't trust the cork...'
> 'I don't know, I don't know...'
> He clapped his hands and at once a barefooted man, stunted and bony, appeared.... (*AD* 10)

Another way in which dialogue is used in *An Area of Darkness* is by alternating it with descriptive one-line sentences. The dialogue becomes one-sided and serves to highlight the internal thought process of the writer and records his response:

> 'You don't want me. You want that officer...'
> I went to him
> 'You have your liquor permit?'
> I showed him the stamped and signed foolscap sheaf.
> 'You have your transport permit?'
> It was the first I had heard of this permit.
> 'You must have a transport permit.'
> I was exhausted, sweating.... (*AD* 18)

Dialogue is also used to narrate the stories of various people that he meets. But here too, the sentences are short and terse and only serve to heighten the tension in the situation at hand. The longer sentences are very few. The longest speech in the Ramnath-Malhotra episode is Malhotra's, wherein he expresses his intentions to the head: "If that is your attitude, sir, then I am sorry to say..." (*AD* 49). All other dialogues are short:

> 'Where is that letter you took this morning?'
> 'It is with Hiralal, Sir.'
> 'And yesterday's letter...'
> Silence.

> 'Where is my letter?'
> 'It is not my job, Sir.' (*AD* 49)

Dialogue is also used to catch the local flavour of English as in the case of Mrs. Mahindra and the people in Kashmir:

> 'Duffer, that Bihari boy.'
> 'I am craze for foreign,' Mrs. Mahindra said.
> 'Just craze for foreign.' (*AD* 85)
>
> 'Two minutes,' he said. 'Three minutes. I fix.' (*AD* 104)
>
> 'Can you swim, Aziz?'
> 'O yes, sahib, I swim.'
> 'Where do you swim?'
> 'Right here on lake'
> 'It must be very cold.'
> 'O no, sahib. Every morning Ali Mohammed and I take off clothes and swim.' (*AD* 155)
>
> 'He is *best* poet'
> 'He is *great* drinker.' (*AD* 132)
>
> Aziz reported, 'He say I overcharge. He say, "Why you tell other sahib I married?" I say, "Why you want secret? Man get married. This is for good. He give party. He invite. He not hide. And why I not tell? You wake up my sahib and he complain."' (*AD* 178)

Dialogue is used in his interaction with the Railway Inspector of Forms and Stationery and in his conversation with Ramchandra Dubey. An IAS officer acted as an interpreter in the latter case so the language used is suitably refined. The use of dialogue in the book is very limited. It is mainly used to set off the writer's own responses or his perception of a situation. The dialogues do not blend into the continuity of the text which mainly comprises of narrated passages. This is in accordance with Naipaul's responses to India as recorded in the book. *An Area of Darkness* is a personal book, the personality and reactions of the author are predominant. The use of dialogue is made in such a way that it enhances the point of view of the writer. The dialogue does not disclose at any stage, the speakers' responses. It is always made to add to the response of the writer.

The use of dialogue in *India: A Wounded Civilization* is very different from that in *An Area of Darkness*. The book is predominantly analytical in tone and dialogue has been very sparingly used. The only instance where direct speech is recorded at some length is in the case of the Prince:

> What keeps a country together? Not economics. Love. Love and affection. That's our Indian way.... You can feed my dog, but he won't obey you. He'll obey me. Where's the economics in that?... Are they happy where you come from? Are they happy in England? (*WC* 34)

Apart from this, the book rests mainly on Naipaul's analysis occasionally punctuated by narrative and descriptive passages. This method is totally inverted in *India: A Million Mutinies Now*. The book abounds in dialogue and dialogue is also used as commentary on a given situation. The writer is totally removed from the reader's view. There are entire sections that are built up on direct speech. A striking example of this is the section in the first chapter that deals with the Bengali film writer. The section begins with a descriptive passage that describes the setting—the one room apartment. This is followed by two pages of direct speech from the Bengali film writer. Thereafter, the author puts in one-line questions which draw more direct speech from the Bengali film writer which runs into another four pages. The same pattern is followed, without exception, throughout the book:

> 'When I first came I had great notion of what a film writer should be. I was wrong then. I thought that a screenplay was close to a novel or a play.... We write visuals—that's what a screen writer is supposed to do....'
>
> 'So now I've been back for a year. The first six months were hard. People were indifferent, because I'd left the club.'
>
> 'Looking back now...don't you think that something might be said for talking a film—as he used to do?'
>
> The writer was unforgiving. 'That is the enemy. That complacent attitude—that is the enemy....'

> 'Who are the nice people in the film business?'
>
> 'Everybody and nobody. It's totally success-oriented....' (*MM* 92)

A comparative study of the use of dialogue in Naipaul's three books on India corresponds to the gradual shift in his sensibility and the growing clarity of his Indian experience. The dialogue in *An Area of Darkness* is not conversational. It carries a touch of confrontation. The near total lack of dialogue in *India: A Wounded Civilization* enhances its analytical tone. The dialogue in *India: A Million Mutinies Now* is predominantly conversational. The voice of the writer enters with the sole purpose of engaging the people in long conversations. The voices of the people build up over the chapters. Each person discloses his/her life and family history. Their stories, handed out in conversations, build up the story of India across generations.

The use of narrative passages serves different purposes in the abovementioned books. Therefore, the narrative passages in each book are different in form and content. In *An Area of Darkness,* the narrative passages are made of long compound sentences. There is a long string of clauses which attempts to put down in words the thoughts that seem to overcrowd the mind of the writer, clamouring for sudden and simultaneous release:

> Bunty comes of a 'good' family, Army, ICS; he might even have princely connexions. He is two or three generations removed from purely Indian India; he, possibly, like his father, has been to an Indian or English public school and one of the two English universities, whose accent, through all the encircling hazards of Indian intonation, he strenuously maintains.... Freed of one set of caste rules, he obeys another, and these are as nice: to introduce Jimmy, whose air-conditioned office is shared and has hard furnishing, into the home of Andy, who has an office to himself with soft furnishings, is to commit a blunder. (*AD* 58-59)

There are numerous such examples throughout the book. These occur mainly when people and places are observed and discussed without having aroused much sentiment from the writer. In situations that trigger off instant rage or disillusionment the sentences that form narrative passages are direct and the number of clauses fewer:

> Mosque on temple: ruin on ruin. This is in the North. In the South there is the great city of Vijayanagar. In the early sixteenth century it was twenty-four miles round. (*AD* 203)
>
> The country had been pillaged before. But continuity had been maintained. With the British, continuity was broken. (*AD* 208)
>
> He was reacting for me, as he had done on the train. But now I knew my hysteria for what it was. The words were his, not mine. They broke the spell. (*AD* 230)

Narrative passages are abundantly used to portray the inner landscape of the author's mind. The sentences are obviously author-centred and run into a series of clauses held together by varied connectives:

> As India had drawn near, I had felt more than the usual fear of arrival. In spite of myself, in spite of lucidity and London and my years, and over and above every other fear, and the memory of the Alexandrian cab-driver, some little feeling for India as the mythical land of my childhood was awakened. (*AD* 42)
>
> Fear made me passionate; it also, I realized later, made me unnaturally convincing. My annoyance was real; when I turned to walk away I was really walking away; when I was prevailed upon to return—easy, since the boatman refused to ferry me back to the road—my fatigue was genuine. (*AD* 102)
>
> It had never rung true to me in Kipling and other writers; and it did not ring true now. Was it the mixture of England and India? Was it my colonial, Trinidad-American, English-speaking prejudice which could not quite accept as real this imposition, without apparent competition, of one culture on another? (*AD* 190)

In this way the mind of the author, overrun with ideas of response to India, finds its narration. Such narrative passages are spread all over the book. Therefore the voice that emerges is predominantly, the voice of the author proclaiming his own reaction to India. The observation is focused not so much on India as on the response it elicits in the author.

India: A Wounded Civilization is totally structured on narrative passages with dialogue and descriptive passages reduced to the barest minimum. A variety of narrative passages give the book its structure. Narrative passages contain the author's commentaries on the literature, society and politics of India. The method used is empirical: observation, analysis, and conclusion:

> About two hundred miles away, still in the south, on a brown plateau of rock and gigantic boulders, are the ruins of the capital city of what was once the great Hindu kingdom of Vijayanagar. (*WC* 14)
>
> To the pilgrims Vijayanagar is its surviving temple. The surrounding destruction is like proof of the virtue of old magic; just as the fantasy of past splendour is accommodated within an acceptance of present squalor. (*WC* 15)
>
> Life goes on, the past continues. After conquest and destruction, the past simply reasserts itself. (*WC* 15)

The same pattern is followed in the narrative passages that deal with people and their ideas. Unlike in *An Area of Darkness,* here Naipaul does not rush into a response or a personal reaction. The situation is laid out before the reader and discussed before Naipaul forwards his thesis:

> At dinner that evening—high up in one of those towers—a journalist, speaking frenetically of many things...touched the subject of identity. 'Indian was a word that was now without a meaning,' he said. (*WC* 70)
>
> For the journalist—though he was an economist and had travelled, and was professionally concerned with change—Indian identity was not something developing or changing

> but something fixed, an idealization of his own background, the past he felt he had just lost. (*WC* 71)

> But it was a middle class burden, the burden of those whose nationalism...required them to have an idea of India. Lower down, in the chawls...needs were more elemental: food, shelter, water, a latrine. Identity there was no problem; it was a discovery. (*WC* 71)

In his analysis of Gandhi and Gandhianism, Naipaul adopts the same strategy. Using a number of examples from contemporary India, Naipaul lays down his thesis for the failure of Gandhianism in India after independence had been won. One such example is Naipaul's use of a statement made by the widow of Jamnalal Bajaj, a dedicated Gandhian:

> Mrs. Bajaj said, she had transferred her loyalty to Vinoba Bhave, the man recognized as Gandhi's successor. 'I walked with Vinobaji for years,' Mrs. Bajaj told Mehta. 'Ten or fifteen miles a day, begging land for the poor. It was very hard...because I never eat anything I haven't prepared with my own hands. Everyone knows that Moslems and Harijans have dirty habits.' (*WC* 156)

> Gandhi swept through India, but he has left it without an ideology. He awakened the holy land; his Mahatmahood returned it to archaism; he made his worshippers vain. (*WC* 159)

In sharp contrast to his first two books on India, the use of narrative passages in *India: A Million Mutinies Now* is concentrated only in the last chapter, 'The House on the Lake: A Return to India.' Other narrative passages are used as beginnings for new ideas or as commentaries on the ideas expressed by the people Naipaul meets or as a remembrance of his first visit to India in 1962. The passages that usher in new ideas mainly deal with factual details and very rarely bring out the personality of the writer or the predominant 'I' of *An Area of Darkness*:

> Calcutta, more than New Delhi, is the British-built city of India. It was one of the early centres of British India; it

> grew with British power, and was steadily embellished; it was the capital of British India until 1930. (*MM* 28)
>
> Culture upon culture now: because the boy who went to La Martinière felt, after his time in Iraq, that part of him was Arab or Iranian. After his classes at La Martinière there were special religious lessons at home everyday.... (*MM* 374)

The narrative passages that deal with the memories of 1962 recur throughout the book. The whole experience of 1962 in retrospect is crystallized in the last chapter:

> The hotel was like a little house. It was called the Hotel Liward.... It had two storeys and a pitched corrugated-iron roof. It stood in its own garden in the lake, not one of the floating gardens...but a fixed plot of earth. (*MM* 492)
>
> It was an extraordinary piece of luck for me. The Liward, my time in Kashmir, became a point of rest in my Indian year, a point of rest in my fearful travelling; and perhaps it enabled me to go through with my Indian venture. (*MM* 492)

The narrative passages towards the end of the book contain Naipaul's altered commentary on India and are a revision of his earlier views:

> What I hadn't understood in 1962, or had taken too much for granted, was the extent to which India had been restored to itself....
>
> In the 130 years or so since the Mutiny—the last 90 years of the British Raj and the first 40 years of independence begin increasingly to appear as part of the same historical period—the idea of freedom had gone everywhere in India.... The liberation of spirit that has come to India could not come as release alone. In India, with its layer below layer of distress and cruelty, it had to come as a disturbance. It had to come as rage and revolt. India was now a country of million little mutinies. (*MM* 517)

Naipaul's use of narrative passages has gradually changed through the course of his three books on India. The narrative passages in *An Area of Darkness* serve chiefly to narrate the thoughts and responses that arise in the mind of the author. The passages in *India: A Wounded Civilization* alternate between factual and analytical content whereas those in *India: A Million Mutinies Now* are mainly reflective. Naipaul has thus developed the narrative passages to serve as keen reflections on the situation at hand. The narrative passages that follow the dialogue are also tempered meditations and are totally different from the indignant outbursts in *An Area of Darkness.*

The descriptive passages in the three books discussed are the only areas in Naipaul's changing technique that have remained unchanged across his journey from *An Area of Darkness* to *India: A Million Mutinies Now.* Although the objects of description keep changing, Naipaul's keen eye for detail does not:

> Kashmir was coolness and colour: the yellow mustard fields, the mountains, snow-capped, the milky blue sky in which we rediscovered the drama of clouds. It was men wrapped in brown blankets against the morning mist, and barefooted shepherd boys with caps and covered ears on steep wet rocky slopes. (*AD* 95)

> Beyond the Bund it was a medieval town, and it might have been of medieval Europe. It was a town, damp or dusty, of smells: of bodies and picturesque costumes discoloured and acrid with grime, of black, open drains...a town of prolific pariah dogs of disregarded beauty...of starved puppies shivering in the damp caked blackness of butchers' stalls...a town of narrow lanes and dark shops and choked courtyards.... (*AD* 123)

> ...a pair of reaping shoes. At the front of the left shoe was a narrow cutting blade; on the right side of the right shoe was a longer curved blade. So the peasant, advancing through his ripe corn, would kick with his left foot and cut, while with his right he would describe a wide arc and cut: a harvest dance. (*WC* 123)

> Apart from this garden, the fort was built up, all paved, no earth showing. Passages, courtyards, terraces, roofs:

> crumbling brick and plaster, more perishable than wood. Here and there were small, oppressive, over-decorated, dark rooms, with dark mirrors on the walls and carved ceilings. (*MM* 466)

> The water of the lake, streaming through my fingers, was cool. And even with all the traffic, the lake still had its spring-time clarity. It was full of little fish, a delight to see, and the ferns at lake bottom tossed slowly in the current. (*MM* 496)

Naipaul's narrative technique, as revealed in his three books on India is directly linked to Naipaul's response to India. In *An Area of Darkness,* the voice of the author is predominant. It is a voice filled with rage and strong reactions. The people Naipaul meets are also absorbed into his larger personal response. The narrative is linear, in the sense that all experiences involve the author and on the basis of his experiences he forwards a thesis on India. In *India: A Wounded Civilization,* the writer's personal response exists but turns more analytical and organized. Naipaul attempts to understand India and identifies the maladies that ail this once glorious country. So it is mainly history that speaks in Naipaul's analysis. Here too, the narrative is linear as Naipaul encounters literature, history and society one after the other. In both these books, a single voice is dominant. It is the voice of the author.

In *India: A Million Mutinies Now,* the narrative is multi-layered. The narrators are numerous and they narrate their own stories. The voice of the author only serves to organise the numerous narratives. In this book Naipaul has been able to establish a kind of link with India. This coming to terms with India led Naipaul to the realization of the plurality and paradox of India. That is why he steps back and lets the narrators speak for themselves. Thus, a million voices speak of a million mutinies. The voice of the author seems to have multiplied itself into numerous narrators. Each narrator discloses a special struggle that had led to a special development. The narrators describe the process of change and all these numerous voices from different parts of the country give a complete picture of India. With *India: A Million*

Mutinies Now, Naipaul overcomes his obsession with his response to India and looks at the country through the eyes of its people. Thus, the Naipaulian shift from the self to the country across twenty-seven years finds its narrative equivalent in his books on India.

7
CONCLUSION

> In 24 years I had succeeded in making a kind of return journey, shedding my Indian nerves, abolishing the darkness that separated me from my ancestral past.
>
> V.S. Naipaul, *India : A Million Mutinies Now.*

Our times are difficult times, times of conflicting ideas and ideals, conflicting realities and divergent visions. Our world bears the mutations of our histories and individuals are largely left on their own, without the support system of society and family. The centre has given way in face of the power politics of human enterprise. V.S. Naipaul continues to record his vision of our times in spite of unsparing criticism from readers and scholars. His works continue to be totally committed to his own vision of the world. He is a writer who can go back to himself and acknowledge a fault or change of vision and a progression in his understanding of his world as and when such a change takes place. In the preceding chapters an attempt has been made to trace this progression in relation to his engagement with India.

Naipaul's writings are inextricably merged with his personal experience and no study on Naipaul can be conducted without taking into account the formative forces behind his literary talent. One such major force was the Hindu-India of the Caribbean in which he was born and brought up. His grandmother's house provided the first link with his Hindu self and with the India of his ancestors. Naipaul grew up with a highly eulogized idea of India. Although he did not understand much about the Hindu rules and rituals of his grandmother's house, there was always something sacred in the very idea of India. He was next introduced to the Hindu India of his father's stories, which epitomized for him the unity of the old world. As he grew, Naipaul observed a chasm between the two worlds that he inhabited. One was the colonial world of Trinidad and the other was the old Hindu world. At the beginning of his career, Naipaul attempted to block out *his* experience of his own society. However he realized that it was out of his experience that his writings would evolve and so he returned to draw on his experience. The same pattern emerges in Naipaul's engagement with India in his three books that have been discussed in the thesis.

Naipaul's first book on India, *An Area of Darkness* was the outcome of his first face-to-face encounter with India. India so far had been to him only an idea—an idea that he had inherited in Trinidad. When faced with the actuality of India, its distress and pain affected Naipaul more strongly than its newly won independence. He could not catch the dominant nationalistic spirit of those times and instead wrote a very personal account of his experiences and disappointments. The India of his dreams, the India of his grandfather was lost forever. The diasporic insecurities began to work and soon transformed into an urge for escape and flight. The book represents the first stage in Naipaul's growth as a writer of the Diaspora because, in this book, Naipaul has marked the areas that created unrest in him. He has marked the areas of pain and squalor of futile mimicry and of degeneration. This marking of the areas was the first step. He also marked the co-existence of opposite and incongruous sensibilities in people. I have shown that *An Area of Darkness* marks his perplexity, his rage and his inability to comprehend the India that meets his eye or its relation to the India of Trinidad.

Amidst the volatile response generated by *An Area of Darkness* certain aspects of Naipaul's sensibility were overlooked. These aspects were the areas wherein Naipaul experienced genuine concern for all that was innocent and uncorrupted in India. Such responses lie scattered throughout the book largely ignored by critics and readers. These areas are the genesis ground for Naipaul's recurrent concerns with India.

Naipaul's second book on India, *India: A Wounded Civilization*, marks the second stage in the progression of his engagement with India. The book is Naipaul's exposition of the problems of India. Here, the areas that Naipaul had marked in *An Area of Darkness* are subjected to extensive scrutiny and the causes behind the pain and squalor and deficiencies of India are found. Naipaul identifies one major cause that is at the root of all maladies that ail India: a deep rupture was caused in the people's idea of themselves by repeated invasions and conquests. The traditional knowledge and talent was systematically destroyed and with the coming of the British, there occurred the final rupture in the sensibilities of the people. Traditional skills and craftsmanship died out. Alien institutions were forced on the people and traditional institutions were so completely destroyed that even after independence, India could not produce even a fragment of the talent, knowledge and expertise that it had possessed in the past.

But then, Naipaul does not stop with a critique of foreign rule. He goes on to hunt for causes from within the Indian fabric that were responsible for India's predicament and comes up with the following conclusions. The concept of nationhood was totally alien to India as India had so far only known a series of rulers in the past. Gandhi mobilized the people of India to an idea of unity by invoking the age-old Indian concept of *dharma*. He infused new meaning in the ideals of service and sacrifice in such a way that the struggle for independence cut across caste and class barriers. Independence was won but the idea of self-governance did not reach the masses. The nameless millions, who had walked behind Gandhi, now returned to their individual worlds and personal interests. Gandhi was thus absorbed into Indian symbolism. Gandhianism became ritualised and lost its ideological content. Indian leadership continued to work on the old British patterns; the British institutions continued to function. However, Naipaul does record development at those places, where he observes a change in the people at the grass-root level. He also sees development in the change that the creation of industries brought about in the lives of the people. By giving the landless poor an alternative to their unending indebtness and poverty, the industries created people who had a new sense of the self and a new morality. In this movement at the bottom of the social ladder lay Naipaul's hope for the regeneration of India.

Naipaul's third book on India, *India: A Million Mutinies Now* marks the third stage in Naipaul's engagement with India. In this book Naipaul has analysed and explained the constructions of his own first response to India. The book is a picture gallery of India. Naipaul has observed India at those places from where regeneration and growth have begun. The book follows a pattern: Individuals are observed, their opinions are recorded and placed against those of the earlier generation. In this way Naipaul traces the process of development. Each character is shown in the capacity in which he has negotiated change and invested in development. By holding these characters against their parents or grandparents, Naipaul sees positive change and growth. Naipaul has also traced a steady growth in the lives of Indian women. Throughout the book, Naipaul has observed womanhood in various forms and also the subtle ways in which it has begun to assert itself. Naipaul also observes the double burden of the home and the workplace that the new Indian woman has to carry. In *India: A Million Mutinies Now*, Naipaul has recorded a chain of voices that proclaim that India is on the move. Naipaul's own voice is mainly restricted to the first and last few pages of the book.

These three books on India fall into a pattern and need to be read in relation to the forces at work within Naipaul the person and Naipaul the writer. Had Naipaul limited himself to empirical observations on India, these books could have been read as commentaries on India. But that is not so; Naipaul has taken these books out of the impersonal realm of commentary by referring to the interiority of his own experience. He has analysed his personal responses to India in terms of his experiences in Trinidad, in terms of his cultural inheritance in his grandmother's house, in terms of his anxieties and fears for his own identity. Therefore the only complete perspective that can be adopted for viewing these books can be the one which takes both of the above mentioned factors into account. The diasporic perspective performs this double function and the books can thus be studied as a diasporic writer's attempt to establish a link with the land of his ancestors.

Naipaul criticism, specially the criticism from India, plays a major role in creating a broader understanding of Naipaul's vision. Naipaul, for Indians is an 'outsider' who cannot be given the right to an insider's knowledge of the country. The outsider ought to be content with observing the glories of India. The very fact that this outsider decides to enter their very personal world of defeat and degeneration is enough to put the insiders on the defensive. The thrust of the attack is not so much on *what* Naipaul observes but on *why* he chooses to observe the obvious poverty of India. He is attacked for having a hidden agenda of lambasting India in his books to win acclaim in the West. The Western scholars and critics complicate matters further by lauding Naipaul for his keen and accurate vision of the problems of India and for his unsentimental approach. This created further resistance among Indian scholars and in the cacophony of attacks and counter-attacks, the content of Naipaul's words was lost. His criticism of India was blown out of proportion; his concern for India was not brought to light. The role of the construction of the writer's sensibility was altogether neglected.

Naipaul's books on India therefore demand a double discernment. Naipaul is to be read in relation to his diasporic status and also in relation to his world vision, which had trained him to look for fissures and lacunae in societies and sensibilities. Before he came to India, he had already evolved his own method of literary exposition of the predicament of the world. His method was that of scathing critique, which he adopted in *An Area of Darkness.* Also at work in *An Area of Darkness* was the confirmation of his own rootlessness. He had never felt rooted in Trinidad, he had grown up to believe that his roots lay in far off India—the sacred land that his grandfather came from. He half expected India to be a pastoral land from a fairy tale. This first book therefore is a very personal book. It is a cry of rage, an attempt to retreat from a reality that is painful. Naipaul's grandfather, when he left India for Trinidad had not carried tales of Indian poverty and pain with him. The reason why he had to indenture himself was never mentioned and in his grandmother's house in

Trinidad, there were no signs of an indentured past, Naipaul's grandfather had carried with him fairy tales of India as a golden land. This kind of selective amnesia is not uncommon in diasporic communities. Naipaul inherited it. This was the main reason why *An Area of Darkness* comes up as a rather confused response to India.

In *India: A Wounded Civilization*, this is changed to a great extent. It is the outcome of Naipaul's declaration in *An Area of Darkness* that he did not want India to sink. The analysis of the problems of India contained in *India: A Wounded Civilization* attempts not only to condemn the devastating enterprise of India's conquerors but also to create a feeling that all is not over yet. That India will go on if certain things are rectified. With this purpose, Naipaul presents his analyses. What he is actually trying to save is not India but his idea of India that *An Area of Darkness* had threatened to take away. Having done that, Naipaul comes out with yet another book, which is very different from the first two. *India: A Million Mutinies Now* is his attempt to establish the long lost connection with India. He is now an insider because the dirt or distress that he sees does not throw him into a spasm of revulsion. He can stand and look beyond what strikes the eye. The squatters' settlements are not longer breeding grounds of disease but areas of mutinies that add momentum to India's journey towards change and promise growth.

The whole unconscious working of the diasporic consciousness is laid out in Naipaul's works and comments on India. Naipaul's comment on India during his visit last winter elucidates this. In 1990, in *India: A Million Mutinies Now* he wrote that his own lack of understanding generated his reactions:

> What I hadn't understood in 1962, or had taken too much for granted, was the extent to which the country had been remade; and even the extent to which India had been restored to itself.... (*MM* 517)

Ten years later on a visit to India, he made the following comment on the intellectual growth in India:

> There is a kind of intellectual life now that didn't exist in the 1960's. India is on the verge of immense intellectual development, I think in every field.[1]

This is a classic example of Naipaul the person and Naipaul the writer, playing hide and seek with each other's experience. It points at the subtle and unconscious ways in which diasporic consciousness works in the interior landscape of the writer's mind. Physical proximity with a situation is no guarantee for directness of experience. It cannot be a measuring rod for authenticity of vision. Vision cannot be limited to the duration of experience either. Vision depends on perspective. With the reworlding that occurred as a result of Imperial rule, the old world unity of vision was shattered and multiple perspectives were generated. It is therefore obvious that perspectives on India would also be different and varied. The resistance generated by Naipaul's vision in India is a clear example of the extent to which the Indian fabric has been wounded. In any perspective that threatens to shatter our idea of ourselves, we see a potential threat to our culture and civilization. Naipaul criticism in India has its own role in exposing the working of the diasporic consciousness in Naipaul. Both follow the same pattern of attempting to block out the experience that threatens the unity of the self. Naipaul attempted to block out India in his first book and India attempted to block out Naipaul. Today both stand changed. Naipaul has progressed towards a better understanding of India and Indian scholars and critics are revising their views on Naipaul. It is a process of coming to terms from both sides. Naipaul has been very candid about this in his process of writing:

> So step by step, book by book, though seeking each time only to write another book, I eased myself into knowledge. To write was to learn. Beginning a book, I always felt I was in possession of all the facts about myself; at the end I was always surprised. The book before always turned out to have been written by a man with incomplete knowledge. (*FC* 27-28)

Naipaul's three books on India record the above process, not only in sensibility but also in style.

An Area of Darkness is full of Naipaul's own comments and reactions. The 'I' of the writer is predominant; *India: A Wounded Civilization* changes this. The text is analytical and arguments are conducted on the basis of what meets the eye rather than what strikes the heart. The style and language are also changed accordingly. In *India: A Million Mutinies Now,* this style is embellished to perfection. The text records directly the voices and experiences of the people Naipaul meets. The writer's observations are reduced to bare minimum. The voices speak for themselves and the judgment is left open to the reader. The writer not only steps back but also explains the cause behind his reactions in his earlier books. In this too, the tone is analytical and expository. Thus Naipaul's books on India present a record of the development of his sensibilities and concerns and the corresponding development of his style.

Naipaul's value in our present world is that of a writer who works amidst the fragmented parts of our history. Over a period of time he has brought to focus our past and present through his own unique vision. His is not a static record but one that progresses and grows through each book. His status as a diasporic writer and the problematic fissure it created in his Indian sensibility has recorded for posterity the deep psychological violence caused by colonial rule and its legacies of confusion, alienation and psychological exile which the world has to continue to live with.

Critics hold divergent views on Naipaul and the number of judgments passed on him are equally numerous. Naipaul continues in spite of those. His only guiding light is his own vision. He has a purpose in what he writes and his being truthful to no vision or idea other than his own makes his enterprise more historically relevant. The past needs to be shaken out of its role of the psychological feel-good resort for bruised reality. Naipaul advocates a critical analysis of the past and for this the past has to be always kept in view while the present is being worked on.

No study on Naipaul and India will be complete without a discussion of the political side of Naipaul's engagement with India. Throughout the course of his encounters with India beginning with *An Area of Darkness,* Naipaul has refused to be contained within the politically correct boundaries that have, of late, come to be assigned to creative writers and intellectuals. The latest example is the way in which the scholars and intellectuals have allowed the Narmada issue to fizzle out and the way in which the media has dealt with the intellectual commitment of people like Medha Patekar and Arundhati Roy. Naipaul's writings and comments on Indian politics are highly charged. By opening a debate on the way we perceive our history and politics, Naipaul has sent across waves of shock among our politicians and journalists who hold a monopoly over political opinion. Pre-independence times are replete with examples of what intellectual commitment can do for a society. Ironically, post-independence times reverberate with the deafening silence of the intellectuals. It is unfortunate that Naipaul's debate is left to the journalists to report and to the politicians who distort it to suit their election propaganda. This is substantiated by the mutilation of Naipaul's comments subsequent to the demolition of the Babri Masjid; calling it an act of balancing of history. Those who are aware of Naipaul's thesis for the marginalized and subjugated people will immediately establish a link between Naipaul's patience with the resurgence among the marginalized in the form of Dalit rebellions. Naipaul sees this kind of violence as a by-product of the marginalized people's coming to the centre. People who have been cheated and oppressed by established institutions for hundreds of years cannot believe in these institutions all of a sudden. So they strike out, hold on to whatever they can lay their hands on. Following the same pattern, the act of demolition, when seen in isolation as a compulsive act on the part of a people whose culture was systematically destroyed was termed "an act of balancing of history" by Naipaul. However, Naipaul is suspicious of Hindu militancy as a systematized form of political ideology and finds it to be a mimicry of Islamic fundamentalism.

Naipaul's opinions are his own but they arise out of a sense of commitment. It is a pity that intellectual commitment has been sidelined and no academic debates emerge out of the ideas generated by those few intellectuals who still choose to voice them. Naipaul's opinions and comments are an example of his continuing intellectual commitment. His changing comments on Hindu nationalism show a progression in the development of his understanding of the use of Hinduism in national politics. Naipaul is a chronicler of our present times. He accepts ideas and ideologies in the form of the present connotations that these have acquired. His books on India should be accepted as diasporic chronicles that attempt to link the past to the present in ways that lead to a progression in his diasporic concerns for India.

Notes and References

CHAPTER 1

1. Salman Rushdie, "Cry my beloved country," *Hindu Magazine* 18 June 2000: VIII.
2. Rushdie VIII.
3. Non-resident dock where indentured Indian labourers were brought.
4. Neena Vyas, "Narayan's homage to labourers of Indian Origin," *Hindu* 12 March 2001: 11.
5. William Safran, "Diasporas in Modern Societies: Myths of Homeland and Return," *Diaspora: A Journal of Transnational Studies,* 1 (Spring 1991): 83-84.
6. Vijay Mishra, "New Lamps for Old: Diasporas Migrancy Border," *Commonwealth Writing: A Study in Expatriate Experience.* Ed. R.K. Dhawan and L.S.R. Krishna Sastry (New Delhi: Prestige Books, 1994) 70.
7. Mishra 71.
8. Ernest Renan, "Qu'est–ce qu'une nation?" *Oeuvres Completes de Ernest Renan* (Paris: Calman-Levy, 1947).
9. Frantz Fanon, *The Wretched of the Earth.* Trans. Constance Farrington (New York: Grove Press, 1963).
10. Benedict Anderson, *Imagined Communities: Reflections on the Origin and Spread of Nationalism* (London: Verso, 1991) 4-6.
11. Farrukh Dhondy, "The Great Indian Diaspora is More Indian than Great," *Outlook* 15 November, 1999: 100-03.
12. Homi Bhabha, *Location of Culture* (London: Routledge, 1994) 2.
13. Homi Bhabha, "DissemiNation: time, narrative, and the margins of the modern nation," *Nation and Narration,* Ed. Homi Bhabha (London: Routledge, 1990) 291. Hereafter abbreviated as *Nation.*
14. Bhabha, *Nation* 320.
15. Edward Said, *Culture and Imperialism* (London: Vintage, 1994) 407.

16. Said 408.
17. V.S. Naipaul, "Conrad's Darkness," *Critical Perspectives on V.S. Naipaul,* Ed. Robert D. Hamner (London: Heinemann, 1997) 56. Hereafter abbreviated as *Critical Perspectives.*
18. Joseph Conrad, *Heart of Darkness And Other Tales.* 1902. Ed. Cedric Watts (Oxford: Oxford UP, 1990) 140-41.
19. Peter Nazareth, "Out of Darkness: Conrad and Other Third World Writers," *Conradiana* 14, No. 3 (1982): 178.
20. Naipaul, *Critical Perspectives* 54-65.
21. Naipaul, *Critical Perspectives* 57.
22. Naipaul, *Critical Perspectives* 57.
23. Naipaul, *Critical Perspectives* 60.
24. George Lamming, *The Pleasures of Exile* (London: Michael Joseph, 1960) 225.
25. Derek Walcott, *The Antilles: Fragments of Epic Memory—The Nobel Lecture* (New York: Farrar, Strauss and Giroux, 1993).
26. V.S. Naipaul, *A House For Mr. Biswas* (New Delhi: Penguin Books India, 1969) 316.
27. K.L. Gillion, *Fiji's Indian Migrants* (Melbourne: Oxford UP, 1962) and J.C. Jha, "Indian Heritage in Trinidad, West Indies," *Caribbean Quarterly* 19, No. 2 (1973): 32-33 have described this phenomenon.
28. Bhikhu Parekh, "Some Reflections on the Indian Diaspora," *Journal of Contemporary Thought* 3 (1993): 106.
29. Sura P. Rath, "Home(s) Abroad: Diasporic Identities in Third Spaces," *Journal of Contemporary Thought,* 9 (Summer 1999): 7-8.
30. Salman Rushdie, *Imaginary Homelands* (London: Granta Books, 1991) 10.
31. Amitav Ghosh, "The Diaspora in Indian Culture," *Public Culture,* 2, No. 1 (1989): 73-78.
32. Chaman Nahal, "E.M. Forster and Ruth Jhabvala," *The New Literatures in English* (New Delhi: Allied, 1985) 66.
33. Salman Rushdie, *Shame* (London: Vintage, 1995) 87-88.
34. Shashi Tharoor, Introduction, *India: From Midnight to the Millennium* (New Delhi: Penguin Books India, 1998) 6.
35. Lavina Melwani, "Home Is Where The Heart Is," *Hindustan Times* 9 January 2000.
36. Melwani, *Hindustan Times.*

37. V.S. Naipaul, *Finding The Centre* (London: Penguin, 1985) 53. Hereafter abbreviated as *FC.*
38. Gillon Aitkin, Introduction, *Letters Between A Father and Son,* by V.S. Naipaul (London: Abacus) ix. Hereafter abbreviated as *Letters.*
39. V.S. Naipaul, *The Enigma of Arrival* (London: Penguin, 1987) 155. Hereafter abbreviated as *EOA.*
40. V.S. Naipaul, *Miguel Street* (London: Penguin, 1971) 165.
41. Victor Ramraj, "The All-Embracing Christlike Vision: Tone and Attitude in *The Mimic Men," Critical Perspectives on V.S. Naipaul,* Ed. Robert D. Hamner (London: Heinemann, 1977) 129.
42. Ian Hamilton, "Without a Place," *Times Literary Supplement* 30 July 1971: 897-98.
43. Alastair Niven, "V.S. Naipaul's Free Statement," *Commonwealth Literature and the Modern World.* Ed. Hena Maes-Jelinek (Brussels: Didier, 1975).
44. V.S. Naipaul, *India: A Million Mutinies Now* (London: Vintage, 1998) 517. Hereafter abbreviated as *MM.*

CHAPTER 2

1. Nissim Ezekiel, "Naipaul's India and Mine," *New Writing in India.* Ed. Adil Jussawala (Baltimore: Penguin,1974) 71-90.
2. C.D. Narasimhaiah, "Somewhere something has snapped," *Literary Criterion* 6, No. 4 (1965): 83-96.
3. H.H. Anniah Gowda, 'Naipaul in India,' *Literary Half Yearly* 11, No. 2 (1970): 163-70.
4. K. Natwar Singh, 'Unhappy Pilgrim,' *New York Times Book Review* 11 July 1965: 35.
5. Helen Tiffin, "The Lost Ones: A Study of the Works of V.S. Naipaul," (Ph.D. diss., Queens University, Kingston, Ontario, 1972) 117.
6. William Walsh, *A Manifold Voice: Studies in Commonwealth Literature* (London: Chatto and Windus, 1970) 64.
7. Sudha Rai has discussed this at length in her book. *V.S. Naipaul: A Study in Expatriate Sensibility* (New Delhi: Arnold Heinemann, 1982) 9-24.
8. Gail Minault, "Through a Glass Darkly: Naipaul's Post-Colonial Travel Accounts," *Osmania Journal of English Studies* (1982) 15.
9. Sara Suleri, "Naipaul's Arrival," *Yale Journal of Criticism* 2, I (Fall 1988): 159.

10. C.D. Narasimhaiah, "Somewhere something has snapped," *Literary Criterion* 6, No. 4 (1965): 95-96.

CHAPTER 3

1. Helga Chaudhary, "V.S. Naipaul's Changing Vision of India: a Study of *An Area of Darkness* and *India: A Wounded Civilization," Literary Half Yearly* 23, No. 1 (January1982): 111.
2. Fawzia Mustafa, *V.S. Naipaul* (Cambridge: Cambridge University Press, 1995): 133.
3. Dilip Chitre, "Naipaul and India 2: For him a Difficult Country," *New Quest* 9 (May-June 1978): 175-86.
4. H.B. Singh, "V.S. Naipaul: A Spokesman for Neo-colonialism," *Literature and Ideology* 2 (Summer 1969): 71-85.
5. Sudha Rai, *V.S. Naipaul: A Study in Expatriate Sensibility* (New Delhi: Arnold Heinemann, 1982).
6. Gordon Rohler, "The Ironic Approach: The Novels of V.S. Naipaul," *The Islands in Between.* Ed. Louis James (London: Oxford University Press, 1968): 139.
7. William Walsh, *V.S. Naipaul* (Edinburgh: Oliver and Boyd, 1973): 76.
8. V.S Naipaul, "V.S. Naipaul in Los Angeles Times—*The Times of India,*" Online. Posted by ashokvc@giasbm01.vsnl.net.in (Sun, 23 June 1996 17: 26: 16 PDT) http://www.freeindia.org/ack (italics mine).
9. V.S. Naipaul, "Christianity didn't damage India like Islam," Interview with Tarun J. Tejpal, *Outlook* 15 November 1999: 59.

CHAPTER 4

1. H.H. Anniah Gowda, "Naipaul in India,"*Literary Half Yearly* 11, No. 2 (1970): 170.
2. William Walsh, *V.S. Naipaul* (Edinburgh: Oliver and Boyd, 1973): 75.

CHAPTER 5

1. Robert William Fogel and G.R. Elton, *Which Road to the Past? Two Views of History* (New Haven: Yale University Press, 1983) 99.
2. Qtd. in Elaine, Jordan, "Enthralment: Angela Carter's Speculative Fictions," *Plotting Change: Contemporary Women's Fiction,* ed., Linda Anderson (London: Edward Arnold, 1999): 19.
3. Jordan 19.

4. Qtd. in Nita Kumar, ed., *Women as Subjects* (New Delhi: Stree, 1994): 6.
5. Kumar 21.

CHAPTER 7

1. Shyam Bhatia, "India needs to come to terms with its past, says Naipaul," *Times of India* 30 October 2000.

Bibliography

I. THE WORKS OF V.S. NAIPAUL

Fiction

Naipaul, V.S. *The Mystic Masseur.* London: André Deutsch, 1957 (Penguin Edition: 1964).

———. *The Suffrage of Elvira.* London: André Deutsch, 1958 (Penguin Edition: 1969).

———. *Miguel Street.* London: André Deutsch, 1959 (Penguin Edition: 1971).

———. *A House for Mr. Biswas.* London: André Deutsch, 1961 (Penguin Edition: 1969).

———. *Mr. Stone and the Knights Companion.* London: André Deutsch, 1963 (Penguin Edition: 1973).

———. *The Mimic Men.* London: André Deutsch, 1967 (Penguin Edition: 1969).

———. *A Flag on the Island.* London: André Deutsch, 1971 (Penguin Edition: 1969).

———. *In a Free State.* London: André Deutsch, 1971 (Penguin Edition: 1973).

———. *Guerrillas.* London: André Deutsch, 1975 (Penguin Edition: 1976).

———. *A Bend in the River.* London: André Deutsch, 1979 (Penguin Edition: 1980).

———. *The Enigma of Arrival.* London: Viking, 1987 (Penguin Edition : 1987).

———. *A Way in the World.* London: Heinemann, 1994.

———. *Half A Life.* London: Picador, 2001.

Non-Fiction

Naipaul, V.S. *The Middle Passage.* London: André Deutsch, 1962 (Penguin Edition: 1969).

———. *An Area of Darkness*. London: André Deutsch, 1964 (Penguin Edition: 1968).

———. *The Loss of El Dorado*. London: André Deutsch, 1969 (Penguin Edition: 1973).

———. *The Overcrowded Barraccoon*. London: André Deutsch, 1972.

———. *India: A Wounded Civilization*. London: André Deutsch, 1977 (Penguin Edition: 1979).

———. *The Return of Eva Peron*. London: André Deutsch, 1980 (Penguin Edition: 1981).

———. *Among the Believers*. London: André Deutsch, 1981 (Penguin Edition: 1982).

———. *Finding the Centre*. London: André Deutsch, 1984 (Penguin Edition: 1985).

———. *A Turn in the South*. London: André Deutsch, 1989.

———. *India: A Million Mutinies Now*. London: William Heinemann, 1990 (Vintage Edition: 1998).

———. *Beyond Belief: Islamic Excursions Among the Converted Peoples*. London: Little, Brown and Company, 1998 (Penguin Edition: 1998).

———. *Letters Between a Father and Son*. London: Little, Brown and Company, 1999 (Abacus Edition: 2000).

Select Interviews

V.S. Naipaul. Interview with Derek Walcott. *The Sunday Guardian* (Trinidad) 7 March 1965: 5, 7.

———. "Without a Place." Interview with Ian Hamilton. *Times Literary Supplement* 30 July 1971: 897-98. Rpt. in *Critical Perspectives*.

———. "Interview with Adrian Rowe-Evans." *Transition* 40 (1971): 56-62. Rpt. in *Quest* 78 (Sept.-Oct. 1972): 47-55.

———. "The Novelist V.S. Naipaul talks about his childhood." *Listener* 7 September 1972: 306.

———. "V.S. Naipaul, Novelist as Thinker." Interview with Alfred Kazin. *New York Times Book Review* 1 May 1977: 7, 20-21.

———. "Meeting V.S. Naipaul." Interview with Elizabeth

Hardwick. *New York Times Book Review* 13 May 1979: 1, 36.

———. "A Conversation With V.S. Naipaul." Interview with Bharati Mukherjee and Robert Boyers. *Salmagundi* 54 (Fall 1981): 4-22.

———. "The Dark Visions of V.S. Naipaul." Interview with Charles Michener. *Newsweek* 16 November 1981: 104-17.

———. "Naipaul at Wesleyan." Interview with M. Banning Eyre. *South Carolina Review* 14 (Spring 1982): 34-47.

———. "A Trip With V.S. Naipaul." Interview with James Applewhite. *Raritan* 10, No. 1 (Summer 1990): 48-54.

———. "I always had to force myself upon the world." Interview with Mohini Kent. *First Quarter* (1997): 59-63.

———. "Religion is often a smokescreen for political oppression." Interview with L.K. Sharma. *Times of India* 1 May 1998: 13.

———. "Christianity didn't damage India like Islam." Interview with Tarun J. Tejpal. *Outlook* 15 November 1999: 48-56.

———. "Hindu revivalists are mimicking Islamic fundamentalists." In conversation with Khushwant Singh. *Outlook* 8 May 2000: 56-59.

Select Articles

V.S. Naipaul. "A Letter to Maria." *New Statesman* 56 (July 1958): 14.

———. "Caribbean Medley." *Vogue* 15 November 1959: 90, 92-93.

———. "Trollope in the West Indies." *The Listener* 15 March 1962: 461.

———. "Tea with an Author." *Bim* 9, No. 34 (Jan.-June 1962): 79-81.

———. "India's Cast-Off Revolution," *Sunday Times* (London) 25 August 1963: 17.

———. "Critics and Criticism." *Bim* 10, No. 38 (Jan.-June 1964): 74-77.

———. "Images." *New Statesman* 24 September 1965: 452-53.

———. "Without a Dog's Chance." *New York Review of Books* 18 May 1972: 29-31.

———. "The Corpse at the Iron Gate." *New York Review of Books* 10 August 1972: 3-7.

———. "How Writing Changes a Writer." *Tapia* 2 December 1973: 1-12.

———. "A Country Dying On Its Feet." *New York Review of Books* 4 April 1974: 21-33.

———. Foreword. *The Adventures of Gurudeva* by Seepersad Naipaul (London: André Deutsch, 1976): 7-23.

———. Introduction. *East Indians in the Caribbean: Colonialism and the Struggle for Identity* (New York: Kraus International Publishers, 1982.

———. "A Note on a Borrowing by Conrad." *New York Review of Books* 16 December 1982: 37-38.

———. "Writing 'A House for Mr. Biswas.'" *New York Review of Books* 24 November 1983: 22-23.

———. "It Is Out of This Violence I've Always Written." *New York Review of Books* 16 September 1984: 45-46.

———. "Among the Republicans." *New York Review of Books* 25 October 1984: 5+.

———. "On Being a Writer." *New York Review of Books* 23 April 1987: 7.

———. "A Million Mutinies." *India Today* 18 August 1997: 36-39.

II. CRITICISM ON V.S. NAIPAUL: BOOKS

Albertazzi, Silvia. *Translating India: Travel and Cross-Cultural Transference in Post-Colonial Fiction in English*. Bologna: Editrice Bologna, 1993.

Amrithanayagam, Guy. *Writers in East-West Encounters: New Cultural Bearings*. London: Macmillan, 1982.

Amur, G.S. and S.K. Desai (eds.). *Colonial Consciousness in Commonwealth Literature*. Bombay: Somaya Publications, 1984.

Baugh, Edward (ed.). *Critics on Caribbean Literature*. London: George Allen and Unwin, 1978.

Boxhill, Anthony. *V.S. Naipaul's Fiction: In Quest of the Enemy.* Fredrickton, N.B.: York Press, 1983.

Braithwaite, E. *Other Exiles.* London: Oxford University Press, 1975.

Cudjoe, Selwyn R. *V.S. Naipaul: A Materialist Reading.* Amherst: University of Massachusetts Press, 1988.

Dhawan, R.K. (ed.). *Commonwealth Fiction.* 3 Vols. New Delhi: Classical Publishing Company, 1988.

Dhawan, R.K. *et al.* (eds.). *Recent Commonwealth Literature.* 2 Vols. New Delhi: Prestige Books, 1989.

Dhawan, R.K. and L.S.R. Krishna Sastry (ed.). *Commonwealth Writing: A Study in Expatriate Experience.* New Delhi: Prestige Books, 1994.

Feder, Lillian. *Naipaul's Truth.* New Delhi: Indialog Publications Pvt. Ltd., 2001.

Gorra, Michael. *After Empire: Scott, Naipaul, Rushdie.* Chicago: University of Chicago Press, 1997.

Gowda, H.H. Anniah. *The Colonial and Neo-Colonial Encounters in Commonwealth Literature.* Mysore: Mysore University Press, 1973.

Griffiths, Gareth. *A Double Exile: African and West Indian Writing Between Two Cultures.* London: Marian Boyars, 1988.

Hamner, Robert D. *V.S. Naipaul.* New York: Twayne Publishers, 1973.

——— (ed.). *Critical Perspectives on V.S. Naipaul.* London: Heinemann, 1977.

Harris, Wilson. *The Womb of Space: The Cross-Cultural Imagination.* Westport C.T.: Greenwood Press, 1983.

———. *The Tradition, the Writer and Society.* Port of Spain: New Beacon, 1967.

Hughes, Peter. *V.S. Naipaul.* London: Routledge, 1988.

Jain, Jasbir. *Problems of Post-Colonial Literatures and Other Essays.* Jaipur: Printwell, 1991.

James, Louis (ed.). *The Islands in Between: Essays on West Indian Literature.* London: Oxford University Press, 1968.

Jameson, Frederic. *The Political Unconscious: Narrative as a Socially Symbolic Act.* London: Methuen, 1981.

Joshi, Chandra B. *V.S. Naipaul: The Voice of Exile.* New Delhi: Sterling, 1994.

Jussawala, Adil (ed.). *New Writing in India.* Baltimore: Penguin, 1974.

King, Bruce. *The New English Literatures—Cultural Nationalism in a Changing World.* New York: St. Martin's Press, 1980.

——— (ed.). *West Indian Literature.* London: Macmillan, 1979.

——— (ed.). *Literatures of the World in English.* London: Routledge, 1974.

Kirpal, Vinay. *The Third World Novel of Expatriation.* New Delhi: Sterling, 1989.

Lamming George. *The Pleasures of Exile.* London: Michael Joseph, 1960.

Mason, Nondita. *The Fiction of V.S. Naipaul.* Calcutta: The World Press Pvt. Ltd., 1986.

McLeod, A.L. (ed.). *Subjects Worthy Fame: Essays on Commonwealth Literature.* New Delhi: Sterling, 1989.

McSweeney, Kerry. *Four Contemporary Novelists: Angus Wilson, Brian Moore, John Fowles, V.S. Naipaul.* Montreal: McGill Queen's University Press, 1983.

Morris, Robert K. *Paradoxes of Order: Some Perspectives on the Fiction of V.S. Naipaul* Missouri: University of Missouri Press, 1975.

Mustafa, Fawzia. *V.S. Naipaul.* Cambridge: Cambridge University Press, 1995.

Narasimhaiah, C.D. (ed.). *Commonwealth Literature: A Handbook of Select Reading Lists.* Delhi: Oxford University Press, 1976.

——— (ed.). *Awakened Conscience: Studies in Commonwealth Literature.* New Jersey: Humanities Press, 1978.

——— (ed.). *Commonwealth Literature: Problems of Response.* Madras: Macmillan, 1981.

Nelson, Emmanuel (ed.). *Reworlding: The Literature of the Indian Diaspora.* New York: Greenwood, 1992.

Newman, Judie. *The Ballistic Bard: Post-Colonial Fiction.* London: Arnold, 1995.

Niven, Atastair (ed.). *The Commonwealth Writer Overseas: Themes of Exile and Expatriation.* Brussels: Didier, 1976.

Nixon, Rob. *London Calling: V.S. Naipaul, Postcolonial Mandarin.* New York: Oxford University Press, 1992.

Pratt, Mary Louis. *Imperial Eyes: Travel Writing and Trans-Culturation.* London: Routledge, 1992.

Rai, Sudha. *Homeless by Choice: Naipaul, Rushdie, Jhabvala.* Jaipur: Printwell, 1992.

———. *V.S. Naipaul: A Study in Expatriate Sensibility.* New Delhi: Arnold Heinemann, 1982.

Ramchand, Kenneth. *The West Indian Novel and Its Background.* New York: Barnes and Noble Inc., 1970.

———. *An Introduction to the Study of West Indian Literature.* London: Faber and Faber, 1976.

Siedel, Michael. *Exile and the Narrative Imagination.* New Haven: Yale University Press, 1986.

Singh, Manjit Inder. *V.S. Naipaul.* Jaipur: Rawat Publications, 1998.

Suleri, Sara. *The Rhetoric of English India.* Chicago: University of Chicago Press, 1992.

Theroux, Paul. *V.S. Naipaul: An Introduction to his Work.* London: André Deutsch, 1972.

Thorpe, Michael. *V.S. Naipaul.* London: Longman, 1976.

Weiss, Timothy. *On the Margins: The Art of Exile in V.S. Naipaul.* Amherst: University of Massachusetts Press, 1992.

White, Landeg. *V.S. Naipaul: A Critical Introduction.* London: Macmillan Press, 1975.

William Walsh. *V.S. Naipaul.* Edinburgh: Oliver and Boyd, 1973.

———. *A Manifold Voice: Studies in Commonwealth Literature.* London: Chatto and Windus, 1970.

III. CRITICISM ON V.S. NAIPAUL: ARTICLES

Amis, Martin. "More Bones," *New Statesman* 4 July 1980: 19-20.

Anderson, Linda R. "Ideas of Identity and Freedom in V.S. Naipaul and Joseph Conrad," *English Studies* 59 (1978): 510-17.

Angrosino, M.B. "V.S. Naipaul and the Colonial Image," *Caribbean Quarterly* 21, Vol. 3 (1975).

Argyle, Barry. "A West Indian Epic," *Caribbean Quarterly* 16, No. 4 (December 1970): 61-69.

Bhabha, Homi. "DissemiNation: time, narrative, and the margins of the modern nation," *Nation and Narration,* Ed. Homi Bhabha (London: Routledge, 1990): 291.

Bhatia, Shyam. "India needs to come to terms with its past, says Naipaul," *Times of India* 30 October 2000.

Bhatia, V.P. "Naipaul's defence of Hindutva," *Organizer* 49, No. 5 (31 August 1997): 13.

Blaise, Clark. "The Commonwealth Writer and His Material," *Awakened Conscience: Studies in Commonwealth Literature.* Ed. C.D. Narasimhaiah. New Delhi: Sterting, 1978.

Boxill, Anthony, "V.S. Naipaul's Starting Point," *Journal of Commonwealth Literature* 10, No. 1 (August 1975): 1-9.

Boyers, Robert, "Confronting the Present," *Salmagundi* 54 (Fall 1981): 77-97.

———. "V.S. Naipaul," *American Scholar* (Summer 1981): 359-67.

Brown, John L. "V.S. Naipaul: A Wager on the Triumph of Darkness," *World Literature* 57, No. 2 (Spring 1983): 223-27.

Brown, Wayne. "On Exile and the Dialect of the Tribe," *Sunday Guardian* (Trinidad), November 8, 1970: 19.

———. "On West Indian Critics and Historians," *Sunday Guardian* (Trinidad), August 23, 1970: 17.

Calder, Angus. "World's End: V.S. Naipaul's *The Mimic Men,*" *The Commonwealth Writer Overseas.* Ed. Alastair Niven. Brussels: Didier, 1976: 271-82.

Campbell, Elaine. "A Refinement of Rage: V.S. Naipaul's *A Bend in the River,*" *World Literature Written in English* 18, No. 2 (November 1979): 394-406.

———. "Beyond Controversy: Vidia Naipaul and Salman Rushdie," *Literary Half-Yearly* 27, No. 2 (1986): 42-49.

Chaudhary, Helga. "V.S. Naipaul's Changing Vision of India: A Study of *An Area of Darkness* and *India: Wounded Civilization*," *Literary Half Yearly* 23, No. 1 (January 1982): 98-114.

Chitre, Dilip. "Naipaul and India 2," *New Quest* 9 (May-June 1978): 174-86.

Coulthard, G.R. "The Literature of the West Indies," *The Commonwealth Pen*. Ed. Alan L. McLeod, New York: Cornell University Press, 1961.

Derrick, A.C. "Naipaul's Technique as a Novelist," *Journal of Commonwealth Literature* 7 (July 1969): 32-44.

Deshpande, Charulata. "Naipaul at Work," *Gentleman* 31 May 1989: 92-106.

Dhondy, Farrukh. "The Great Indian Diaspora is More Indian than Great," *Outlook*, November 15, 1999: 100-03.

Dulai, Surjit S. "The Ganges flows through Africa: V.S. Naipaul's India and *A Bend in the River*," *Journal of South Asian Literature* 26 (1991): 303-21.

Enright, D.J. "The Sensibility of V.S. Naipaul: Who is India?" *Man Is an Onion*, Ed. D.J. Enright. Illinois: Library Press, 1973.

Ezekiel, Nissim. "Wounded and Doomed?" *Debonair* VII, No. 15 (May 1978).

———. "Naipaul's India and Mine." Ed. Adil Jussawala. Baltimore: Penguin, 1974.

Ghosh, Amitav. "The Diaspora in Indian Culture," *Public Culture*, 2, No. 1 (1989): 73-78.

Goodheart, Eugene. "V.S. Naipaul's Mandarin Sensibility," *Partisan Review* 50.2 (1983): 244-56.

Gordimer, Nadine. "White Expatriates and Black Mimics: *In a Free State*," *New York Times Book Review* 17 October 1971: 5, 20.

Gowda, H.H. Anniah. "India in Naipaul's Artistic Consciousness," *The Literary Half-Yearly* 16, No. 1 (January 1975): 27-39.

_____. "Naipaul in India." *Literary Half-Yearly,* 11, No. 2 (1970): 163-70.

Gurnah, Abdulrazak. "V.S. Naipaul and the Nihilism of Primitive People," *Times Literary Supplement* May 20, 1994.

Gussow, Mel. "Writer Without Roots," *New York Times Magazine* 26 December 1976: 8-9, 18-19, 22.

Gurr, A.J. "Third World Novels: Naipaul and After," *Journal of Commonwealth Literature* 7, No. 1 (June 1972): 6-13.

Jacinto, Leela. "Such a long journey," *Sunday Times of India Review* 20 February 2000: 1.

Jain, Jasbir. "Cultural Relativism and Perspective: Naipaul, Chaudhuri and Forster," *Jadavpur Journal of Comparative Literature* 28 (1989-90): 17-26.

Jha, J.C. "Indian Heritage in Trinidad, West Indies," *Caribbean Quarterly* 19, No. 2 (1973): 32-33.

Johnstone, Richard. "Politics and V.S. Naipaul," *Journal of Commonwealth Literature* 14, No. 1 (August 1979): 100-08.

Kapadia, Novy. "In Search of Order: A Study of V.S. Naipaul and Attia Hosain," *Commonwealth Writing: A Study in Expatriate Experience.* Ed. R.K. Dhawan, L.S.R. Krishna Sastry. New Delhi: Prestige Books, 1994: 113-19.

King, Bruce. "V.S. Naipaul," *West Indian Literature.* Ed. Bruce King. London: Macmillan, 1979: 161-78.

_____. "Recent Commonwealth Fiction," *Sewanee Review* 85 (1977): 126-34.

_____. "Ethnicity as Response: Richler, Achebe and Naipaul," *Commonwealth Literature: Themes and Techniques.* Ed. P.K. Rajan *et al.* (Delhi: Ajanta, 1993): 1-13.

King, Lloyd. "The Trauma of Naipauland," *Trinidad Guardian,* September 24, 1967: 16-19.

Kirkler, Bernard. "V.S. Naipaul's *A House for Mr. Biswas,*" *The Listener,* February 13, 1964: 270-71.

Kothandaraman, Bala. "The Writer in Quest of a History: The Case of V.S. Naipaul," *Literary Half-Yearly* 31, No. 1 (1990): 37-48.

Kutty, K. Narayan. "Naipaul and India 1," *New Quest* 9 (May-June 1978): 167-73.

Lelyveld, Joseph. "For Naipaul a Difficult Country," *New York Times Book Review* 12 June 1977: 10, 44.

MacDonald, Bruce. "Symbolic Action in Three of V.S. Naipaul Novels," *Journal of Commonwealth Literature* 9, No. 3 (April 1975): 41-52.

Maes-Jelinek, Hena. "V.S. Naipaul: A Commonwealth Writer?" *Revue de Langues Vivantes* 33 (1967): 499-513.

———. "The Myth of El Dorado in the Caribbean Novel," *Journal of Commonwealth Literature* 6, No. 1 (June 1971): 113-28.

Miller, Karl. "Naipaul's Emergent Country," *The Listener* 28 September 1967: 402-03.

_____. "V.S. Naipaul and the New Order," *Kenyon Review.* 29 (November 1967): 685-98.

Minault, Gail. "Through a Glass Darkly: Naipaul's Post-Colonial Travel Accounts," *Osmania Journal of English Studies* (1982).

Mishra, Vijay. "New Lamps for Old: Diasporas Migrancy Border," *Commonwealth Writing: A Study in Expatriate Experience.* Eds. R.K. Dhawan and L.S.R. Krishna Sastry (New Delhi: Prestige Books, 1994): 70.

Nahal, Chaman. "E.M. Forster and Ruth Jhabvala," *The New Literatures in English* (New Delhi: Allied, 1985): 66.

Naik, M.K. "Two Uses of Irony: V.S. Naipaul's *The Mystic Masseur* and R.K. Narayan's *The Guide,*" *World Literature Written in English* 17, No. 2 (November 1978): 646-55.

Nandkumar, Prema. "V.S. Naipaul," *The Glory and the Good.* New Delhi: Asia Publishing House, 1965.

Nazareth, Peter. "Out of Darkness: Conrad and Other Third World Writers," *Conradiana* 14, No. 3 (1982).

Neill, Michael. "Guerrillas and Gangs: Frantz Fanon and V.S. Naipaul," *Ariel* 13, No. 4 (October 1982): 21-61.

Niven, Alastair. "V.S. Naipaul's Free Statement," *Commonwealth Literature and the Modern World.* Ed. Hena Maes-Jelinek. Brussels: Didier, 1975: 69-78.

———. "Crossing the Black Waters: Nirad C. Chaudhuri's *A Passage to England* and V.S. Naipaul's *An Area of Darkness,*" *Ariel* 9, No. 3 (July 1978): 21-36.

Nunez-Harrell, Elizabeth. "Lamming and Naipaul: Some Criteria for Evaluating the Third World Novel," *Contemporary Literature* 19, No. 1 (1978): 26-47.

Parrinder, Patrick. "V.S. Naipaul and the Uses of Literacy," *Critical Quarterly* 21, No. 2 (Summer 1979): 5-13.

Patterson, John. "Challenging CLR and the Naipauls," *Sunday Guardian* (Trinidad), October 18, 1970: 7+.

Raghvacharyulu, D.V.K. "Naipaul and Narayan: The Sense of Life," *Awakened Conscience*. Ed. C.D. Narasimhaiah. New Jersey: Humanities Press, 1978: 216-25.

Ramchand, Kenneth. "A House for Mr. Biswas," *An Introduction to the Study of West Indian Literature*. Kingston, Jamaica: Nelson Caribbean: 1976: 73-90.

Ramraj, Victor J. "Diminishing Satire: A Study of V.S. Naipaul and Mordecai Richler," *Awakened Conscience*. Ed. C.D. Narasimhaiah. New Jersey: Humanities Press, 1978: 261-74.

_____. "The All-Embracing Christlike Vision: Tone and Attitude in *The Mimic Men*," *Critical Perspectives On V.S. Naipaul*. Ed. Robert D. Hamner. London: Heinemann, 1977.

Rao, K.I. Madhusudana. "V.S. Naipaul's Guerillas: A Fable of Political Innocence and Experience," *Journal of Commonwealth Literature* 14, No. 1 (August 1979): 90-99.

Rao, Susheela N. "Darkness Visible: The Emerging Portrait of India in Naipaul's Updated Travelogue," *Literary Half-Yearly* 38, No. 1 (Jan. 1997): 28-41.

Robinson, Andrew. "The Elusive Genius," *Illustrated Weekly of India* 5 July 1987: 9-15.

Rohlehr, Gordon. "The Ironic Approach: The Novels of V.S. Naipaul," *The Islands in Between*. Ed. Louis James. London: Oxford University Press, 1968.

Russel, John. "No Guides Need Apply: Locating the Non-fiction Novel," *University of Toronto Quarterly* 59, No. 3 (Spring 1999).

Sharma, T.R.S. "Chinua Achebe and V.S. Naipaul: One Version and Two Postures on Post-Colonial Societies," *The Colonial and Neo-Colonial Encounters in Commonwealth Literature*. Ed. H.H. Anniah Gowda. Mysore: Prasaranga, 1983: 82-93.

Shenker, Israel. "V.S. Naipaul, Man Without a Society," *New York Times Book Review*, October 17, 1971: 4.

Singh, H.B. "V.S. Naipaul: A Spokesman for Neo-colonialism," *Literature and Ideology* 2 (Summer 1969): 71-85.

Srinath, C.N. "Crisis of Identity: Assertion and Withdrawal in Naipaul and Arun Joshi," *Literary Criterion* 14, No. 1 (1979): 31-41.

Stokes, Eric. "Images of India," *The Times Literary Supplement*, 3 February 1978.

———. "The High Caste Defector," *The Times Literary Supplement*, 21 October, 1977.

Sudama, Trevor. "Defending CLR and the Naipauls," *Sunday Guardian* (Trinidad) November 1, 1970: 5.

Subrahmanian, N. "Gandhi—An Intellectual Assessment," *Quest* (Nov./Dec. 1975).

Suleri, Sara. "Naipaul's Arrival," *Yale Journal of Criticism* 2, I (Fall 1988).

Tiffin, Helen. "The Lost Ones: A Study of the Works of V.S. Naipaul," (Ph.D. diss., Queens University, Kingston, Ontario, 1972): 117.

_____. "V.S. Naipaul's 'Outposts of Progress,'" *World Literature Written in English* 22, No. 2 (Autumn 1983).

Tharoor, Shashi. Introduction. *India: From Midnight to the Millennium* (New Delhi: Penguin Books India, 1998): 6.

Thieme, John. "Apparitions of Disaster: Brontëan Parallels in Wide Sargasso Sea and Guerillas," *Journal of Commonwealth Literature* 14, No. 1 (August 1979): 116-32.

———. "V.S. Naipaul's Third Word: A Not so Free State," *Journal of Commonwealth Literature* 10, No. 1 (August 1975): 10-22.

Towers, Robert. "India's Long Night," *The New York Review of Books* XXIV, No. 12 (July 14) 1977.

Wade, C. Alan. "The Novelist as Historian," *The Literary Half-Yearly* 11, No. 2 (1970): 179-84.

Walcott, Derek. "The Achievement of V.S. Naipaul," *Sunday Guardian* (Trinidad) April 12, 1964: 15.

———. "Is V.S. Naipaul an Angry Young Man?" *Trinidad Guardian* August 6, 1967.

Walsh, William. "V.S. Naipaul," *The Literary Criterion* 10 (Summer 1972): 23-37.

Weiss, Timothy. "V.S. Naipaul's "Fin de Siècle": *The Enigma of Arrival* and *A Way in the World*," *Ariel* 27, No. 3 (July 1996): 107-24.

Woodcock, George. "Two Great Commonwealth Novelists: R.K. Narayan and V.S. Naipaul," *Sewanee Review* 87 (1979).

———. "V.S. Naipaul and the Politics of Fiction," *Queen's Quarterly* 87, No. 4 (Winter 1980): 679-92.

Wyndham Francis. "V.S. Naipaul," *The Listener*, October 7, 1971: 461-62.

———. "Writing is Magic," *Trinidad Guardian*, November 15, 1968.

IV. GENERAL BOOKS AND ARTICLES

Achebe, Chinua. *Morning Yet on Creation Day*. New York: Doubleday, 1975.

Ahmad, Aijaz. *In Theory: Classes, Nations, Literatures*. Bombay: Oxford University Press, 1993.

Ananthmurthy, U.R. *Samskara*. Trans. A.K. Ramanujan. New Delhi: Oxford University Press, 1979.

Anderson, Benedict. *Imagined Communities: Reflections on the Origin and Spread of Nationalism*. London: Verso, 1983.

Anderson, Linda (ed.). *Plotting Change: Contemporary Women's Fiction*. London: Edward Arnold, 1999.

Ashcroft, Bill, Gareth Griffiths, and Helen Tiffin (eds.). *The Empire Writes Back: Theory and Practice in Post-Colonial Literatures*. London: Routledge, 1989.

Bakhtin, M. *The Dialogic Imagination*. Austin: University of Texas Press, 1981.

Balibar, Etienne and Immanuel Wallestein. *Race, Nation, Class: Ambiguous Indentities*. London: Verso, 1991.

Berthoff, Warner. *Fictions and Events*. New York: Dutten, 1979.

Bhabha, Homi K. *The Location of Culture*. London: Routledge, 1994.

——— (ed.). *Nation and Narration*. London: Routledge, 1990.

Boechmer, Elleke. *Colonial and Post Colonial Literature: Migrant Metaphors*. Oxford: Oxford University Press, 1995.

Bondurant, Joan V. *Conquest of Violence: The Gandhian Philosophy of Conflict*. London: Oxford University Press, 1959.

Brantlinger, P. *The Rule of Darkness: British Literature and Imperialism 1830-1914*. Ithaca: Cornell University Press, 1988.

Brennan, Timothy. *Salman Rushdie and the Third-World*. London: Macmillan, 1989.

Brown, Judith, *M. Gandhi's Rise to Power*. London: Cambridge University Press, 1972.

Byron, Robert. *The Road to Oxiana*. 1937. New York: Oxford University Press, 1982.

Chaudhary, Nirad C. *Autobigraphy of an Unknown Indian*. 1951. Bombay: Jaico Books, 1971.

Conrad, Joseph. *Heart of Darkness And Other Tales*. 1902. Ed. Cedric Watts (Oxford: Oxford University Press; World's Classics, 1990).

Coulthard, G.R. *Race and Colour in Caribbean Literature*. London: Oxford University Press, 1962.

Dabydeen, David. *The Black Presence in English Literature*. Manchester: Manchester University Press, 1985.

Dange, S.A., Hiren Mukherjee, S.G. Sardesai and Mohit Sen. *The Mahatma*. 1969. New Delhi: People's Publishing House, 1977.

Dhondy, Farrukh. "The Great Indian Diaspora is More Indian Than Great," *Outlook* 15 November 1999: 100-03.

Docherry, Thomas. *Postmodernism: A Reader*. Harvester: Hemel Hampstead, 1992.

Donald James and Ali Rattansi (eds.). *Race Culture and Difference*. London: Open University Press, 1992.

Eagleton Terry. *Exiles and Emigrès*. London: Chatto and Windus, 1970.

Eagleton Terry, Fredric Jameson and Edward Said. *Nationalism Colonialism and Literature.* Minneapolis: University of Minnesota Press, 1990.

Erikson, Erik H. *Gandhi's Truth.* 1969. London: Faber and Faber, 1970.

Fanon, Frantz. *Black Skins, White Masks.* 1952. London: Pluto Press, 1980.

———. *Studies in a Dying Colonialism.* 1959. Harmondsworth: Penguin, 1970.

———. *The Wretched of the Earth.* 1961. Trans. Constance Farrington. New York: Grove Press, 1963.

Fogel, Robert William and G.R. Elton. *Which Road to the Past? Two Views of History.* New Haven: Yale University Press, 1983.

Foucault, Michel. *The Archaeology of Knowledge.* Trans. A. Sheridan. New York: Pantheon, 1972.

———. *The Order of Things.* Trans. A. Sheridan. New York: Random House, 1970.

———. *Discipline and Punish.* Trans. A. Sheridan. New York: Pantheon.

———. *Madness and Civilization.* Trans. R. Howard. New York: Pantheon, 1965.

Gellner, Ernest. *Nations and Nationalism.* Ithaca: Cornell University Press, 1983.

Gilkes, Michael. *The West Indian Novel.* Boston: Twayne, 1981.

Gillion, K.L. *Fiji's Indian Migrants.* Melbourne: Oxford UP, 1962.

Goldberg, David Theo (ed.). *Multiculturalism: A Critical Reader.* London: Blackwell, 1994.

Goonatilake, Susantha. *Crippled Minds: An Exploration into Colonial Culture.* Bombay: Vikas, 1982.

Guha, Ranajit (ed.). *Subaltern Studies,* Vol. I and II—*Writings on South Asian History and Society.* Delhi: Oxford University Press, 1982 and 1983.

Gurr, Andrew. *Writers in Exile: The Creative Use of Home in Modern Literature.* Sussex: The Harvester Press, 1981.

Gutting, Gary. *The Cambridge Companion to Foucault.* Cambridge: Cambridge University Press, 1994.

Haley, Alex. *Roots.* London: Picador, 1976.

Hobsbawm, E.J. *The Age of Empire.* London: Weidenfield and Nicholson, 1987.

———. *Nations and Nationalisms Since 1780: Programme, Myth, Reality.* Cambridge: Cambridge University Press, 1990.

———. *The Age of Extremes: A History of The World 1914-1991.* New York: Pantheon Books, 1994.

Howe, Irving. *Politics and the Novel.* Paris: Menton, 1967.

Hulme, Peter (ed.). *Post-Colonial Theory and Colonial Discourse.* Manchester: Manchester University Press, 1993.

———. *Colonial Encounters: Europe and the Native Caribbean 1492-1797.* London: Methuen, 1986.

Huttenback, Robert A. *Gandhi in South Africa.* Cornell University Press, 1971.

James, C.L.R. *Spheres of Existence.* London: Allison and Busby, 1980.

Kakar, Sudhir. *The Inner World.* New Delhi: Oxford University Press, 1978.

K'ımar, Nita (ed.). *Women as Subjects.* New Delhi: Stree, 1994.

Kundera, Milan. *The Art of the Novel.* 1988. Delhi: Rupa, 1995.

La Guerre, John (ed.). *Calcutta to Caroni: The East Indians of Trinidad.* London: Longman Caribbean, 1974.

Lamming George. *Natives of My Person.* 1972. London: Picador, 1974.

———. *In the Castle of My Skin.* 1953. London: Longman, 1979.

Lannoy, Richard. *The Speaking Tree.* London: Oxford University Press, 1971.

Lyotard, Jean-Francois. *The Post Modern Condition: A Report on Knowledge.* Manchester: University of Manchester Press, 1979.

Mackenzie John. *Propaganda and Empire.* Manchester: Manchester University Press, 1984.

Mahmood, M.M. *The Colonial Encounter.* London: Rex Collins, 1977.

Malgaonkar, Manohar. *The Prince.* New Delhi: Orient Paperbacks, 1970.

Malik, Yogendra, K. *East Indians in Trinidad.* London: Oxford University Press, 1971.

Mannoni, O. *Prospero and Caliban: The Psychology of Colonization.* New York: Praeger, 1964.

Mehta, Ved. *Mahatma Gandhi and his Apostles.* New Delhi: Indian Book Company, 1977.

Melwani, Lavina. "Home Is Where The Heart Is," *Hindustan Times* 9 January 2000.

Memmi, Albert. *The Colonizer and the Colonized.* New York: Orion Press, 1965.

Mills, Sara. *Discourses of Difference.* London: Routledge, 1991.

Moi, Toril. *Sexual/Textual Politics: Feminist Literary Theory.* London: Methuen, 1987.

Mukherjee, Hiren. *Gandhiji.* 1958. New Delhi: People's Publishing House, 1960.

Naipaul, Seepersad. *The Adventures of Gurudeva and Other Stories.* London: André Deutsch, 1976.

Nandy, Ashis. *The Intimate Enemy: Loss and Recovery of Self Under Colonialism.* New Delhi: Oxford University Press, 1983.

Narasimhaiah, C.D. *The Function of Criticism in India.* Mysore: Central Institute of Indian Languages, 1986.

Narayan, R.K. *The Vendor of Sweets.* 1967. Mysore: Indian Thought Publications, 1976.

———. *Mr. Sampath.* 1949. Mysore: Indian Thought Publications, 1973.

Narayan, Shriman (ed.). *The Selected Works of Mahatma Gandhi.* Ahmedabad: Navjivan Publishing House, 1968.

Ngugi Wa Thiong'O. *Homecoming: Essays on African and Caribbean Literature, Culture and Politics.* London: Heinemann, 1972.

———. *Writers in Politics.* London: Heinemann, 1981.

———. *Decolonizing the Mind: The Politics of Language in African Literature.* London: James Curry, 1986.

Parekh, Bhikhu. "Some Reflections on the Indian Diaspora," *Journal of Contemporary Thought* 3 (1993).

Press, John (ed.). *Commonwealth Literature.* London: Heinemann, 1965.

Rath, Sura P. "Home(s) Abroad: Diasporic Identities in Third Spaces," *Journal of Contemporary Thought* 9 (Summer 1999).

Renan, Ernest. *Oeuvres Completes de Ernest Renan.* Paris: Calman-Levy, 1947.

Rushdie, Salman. *Imaginary Homelands: Essays and Criticism 1981-1991.* London: Granta, 1991.

———. *Shame.* London: Vintage, 1995.

———. "A Fantasy Called India." *India Today* 18 August 1997: 58-61.

———. "There's Not Much Support from India." Interview with Farrukh Dhondy. *Outlook* 15 November 1999: 220-22.

———. "Cry my beloved country," *Hindu Magazine* 18 June 2000: VIII.

———. "The Indian Writer in England," *Eye of the Beholder: Indian Writing in English.* Ed. M. Butcher. London: Commonwealth Institute, 1983: 75-83.

Rhys, Jean. *Wide Sargasso Sea.* Harmondsworth: Penguin Books, 1968.

Safran, William. "Diasporas in Modern Societies: Myths of Homeland and Return," *Diaspora: A Journal of Transnational Studies* 1 (Spring 1991).

Said, Edward. *Orientalism.* 1978. Harmondsworth: Penguin, 1995.

———. *The World, the Text and the Critic.* London: Faber, 1984.

———. *Culture and Imperialism.* 1993. London: Vintage, 1994.

Sherlock, Philip M. *West Indies.* London: Thames and Hudson Ltd., 1966.

Soyinka, Wole. *Myth Literature and the African World.* Cambridge: Cambridge University Press, 1976.

Spivak, Gayatri. *In Other Words: Essays in Cultural Politics.* London: Methuen, 1987.

———. *The Post Colonial Critic: Interviews, Strategies, Dialogues.* New York: Routledge, 1990.

Swinden, Patrick. *Unofficial Selves: Character in the Novel from Dickens to the Present Day.* New York: Barnes and Noble, 1973.

Tandon, Prakash. *Punjabi Century.* New Delhi: Orient Paperbacks, 1961.

Tendulkar, Vijay. *Sakharam Binder.* Trans. Shanta Shahane and Kumud Mehta. New Delhi: Hind Pocket Books, 1973.

———. *The Vultures.* Trans. Priya Adarkar. New Delhi: Hind Pocket Books, 1974.

Tharoor, Shashi. *India: From Midnight to the Millenium.* New Delhi: Penguin Books India, 1998.

Tinker, Hugh. *A New System of Slavery.* London: Oxford University Press, 1974.

Tomlinson, John. *Cultural Imperialism.* London: Pinter, 1991.

Viswanathan, Gauri. *Masks of Conquest: Literary Study and British Rule in India.* London: Faber and Faber, 1990.

Vyas, Neena. "Narayan's Homage to Labourers of Indian Origin," *Hindu* 12 March 2001: 11.

Walcott, Derek. *The Antilles: Fragments of Epic Memory—The Nobel Lecture.* New York: Farrar, Strauss and Giroux, 1993.

Weber, Max. *The Religion of India.* 1958. New York: The Free Press, 1968.

Williams, Raymond. *Culture and Society 1780-1950.* London: Chatto and Windus, 1958.

Young, J.C. *Colonial Desire: Hybridity in Theory, Culture and Race.* London: Routledge, 1995.

Index